INTRODUCTION TO THE AMERICAN LEGAL SYSTEM AND CRIMINAL LAW

Legal English and Legal Education

SÉRIE ESTUDOS JURÍDICOS: TEORIA DO DIREITO E FORMAÇÃO PROFISSIONAL

Kauana Vieira da Rosa Kalache

Rua Clara Vendramin, 58 . Mossunguê . Cep 81200-170 . Curitiba . PR . Brasil
Fone: (41) 2106-4170 . www.intersaberes.com . editora@intersaberes.com

Conselho editorial Dr. Ivo José Both (presidente), Drª Elena Godoy, Dr. Neri dos Santos, Dr. Ulf Gregor Baranow ▪ **Editora-chefe** Lindsay Azambuja ▪ **Gerente editorial** Ariadne Nunes Wenger ▪ **Assistente editorial** Daniela Viroli Pereira Pinto ▪ **Preparação de originais** Camila Rosa ▪ **Edição de texto** Monique Francis Fagundes Gonçalves ▪ **Capa** Luana Machado Amaro ▪ **Projeto gráfico** Mayra Yoshizawa ▪ **Diagramação e designer responsável** Luana Machado Amaro ▪ **Iconografia** Regina Claudia Cruz Prestes

Dados Internacionais de Catalogação na Publicação (CIP)
(Câmara Brasileira do Livro, SP, Brasil)

Kalache, Kauana Vieira da Rosa
  Introduction to the american legal system and criminal law: legal English and legal education/Kauana Vieira da Rosa Kalache. Curitiba: InterSaberes, 2021. (Série Estudos Jurídicos: Teoria do Direito e Formação Profissional)

  Bibliografia.
  ISBN 978-65-5517-817-3

  1. Crimes (Direito penal) 2. Direito penal 3. Processo penal 4. Sistema jurídico – Estados Unidos I. Título. II. Série.

20-45476   CDU-343(73)

Índices para catálogo sistemático:
1. Sistema judiciário: Estados Unidos: Direito penal 343(73)
Cibele Maria Dias – Bibliotecária – CRB-8/9427

1ª edição, 2021.

Foi feito o depósito legal.

Informamos que é de inteira responsabilidade da autora a emissão de conceitos.

Nenhuma parte desta publicação poderá ser reproduzida por qualquer meio ou forma sem a prévia autorização da Editora InterSaberes.

A violação dos direitos autorais é crime estabelecido na Lei n. 9.610/1998 e punido pelo art. 184 do Código Penal.

Table of contents

11 ▪ *Presentation*
13 ▪ *Introduction*

Chapter 1
17 ▪ **Comprehending the system and communicating**
19 | The US Legal System
22 | The sources of law
26 | The US Legal Structure
37 | The US Legal Education and Law School Life
44 | Law firms structure and practice areas
46 | Persons and documents in Court
50 | Using the correct verbs and court vocabulary
55 | Communicating
57 | Important advise, explanation and negotiation expressions

Chapter 2
65 ▪ **Working with the case method**
66 | The case method
69 | Legal issues
84 | Briefing cases
89 | Argument strategies

Chapter 3
97 ▪ Legal writing
99 | Writing well
106 | Writing persuasively
115 | Legal drafting
118 | Document designing
120 | Writing methods

Chapter 4
123 ▪ Introduction to the American Criminal System
124 | Introduction to criminal law
150 | Introduction to criminal procedure: pre-trial process
157 | Plea bargaining
170 | Introduction to criminal procedure: trial process
176 | Constitutional Principles regarding criminal procedure
188 | Prison policies

213 ▪ *Conclusion*
217 ▪ *References*
227 ▪ *About the author*

To Georges.

I would like to thank my family, for all the love, support and encouragement, which are their main characteristics.

To all my academic and professional partners, for sharing the knowledge and also for being enthusiastic of my work.

To my partner in life, Georges, for helping me perusing my goals.

To my daughter, Georgia, who inspires me daily, for always arising the best in me.

Finally, I would like to thank those who I have met around the world, in my search for "thinking outside the box", whose dreams were bigger, unfitting their original places – such as mine. Here they are represented by Camila, Beatriz, Vic, Anna Valéria, Constance, Perrine, Goya, Chelsea and Amanda, who were responsible for making my journey more pleasant, the pain more bearable and the tears less frequent. Family can also be chosen.

Presentation

This book mixes theory and the author's experience regarding legal English, the academic life in one of the greatests law schools in United States of America and the American criminal justice system.

In here, the reader will find guidance when it comes to communicating in English in a legal environment, with chapters discussing communication (written and verbal), attorney/client orientation, verb use, among other skills. The reader can also count on great court language lessons.

Furthermore, the book brings a session relating to legal writing guidance and tips, based on the thoughts of the great author Bryan A. Garner on the matter. The analysis made goes from teaching how to build an effective outline to creating a strong argument, facing counterarguments that may be raised – observing the dialectical method, in a pleasant, objective and coherent text.

Finally, the book brings an introduction to the American criminal justice system, discussing the criminal law, the procedure rules and their language, also analyzing some aspects of the law practice in the country.

The reader is invited to a journey, to understanding different ways of practicing the law and comprehending the legal system. Most of the communicating skills discussed in here should be applied, no matter the legal system we are inserted in.

Introduction

I have been submitted to the study of the English language since I got to the school age. Both of my older sisters were English as second language professors, and both of them had lived abroad when I was very young. The English language was common at my home environment, as was music from American, English and Australian singers and bands. My older sisters would spend many time correcting my pronunciation at any attempt of singing Alanis Morissette, Jewel, The Cranberries, Pink Floyd and Simon & Garfunkel – just to name a few.

At the age of 15, I started myself to teach English, as a way of making my own money, in a desperate teenager search for independency. In Brazil, not a lot of people were fluent English speakers at that time, and the search for in company classes – designated to businessman – and classes for kids and teenagers was getting bigger.

After law school, I decided to pursue an international degree in law, at an American university, and after being accepted to the school I really wanted to go to, a huge fear took over me. I knew how to speak and understand the English language, but would I be able to do that in an academic environment? Worse than that, I knew absolutely nothing about the legal English language.

A few months before travelling to the United States (US) and starting classes at University of California, Los Angeles (UCLA), I engaged in a desperate journey seeking a legal English professor or course that could introduce me to that language. The search did not lead to the best outcome; I did not find what I was looking for, even though I spent a lot of money in the search for it.

I got to law school, everything was beautiful, staff was gentle and kind, campus tours, welcoming brunches, sunset toasts with beer and wine in the law schoolyard and classes finally started. After one week of seminars, I went back to my rented apartment and cried in the middle of the living room floor.

The only thought in my head was: "What the hell was I thinking? I cannot do this!". Classes were crowded; professors spoke extremely fast, and the language? That was not English, for Christ's sake! I did not know what language they were speaking, but that was definitely not English! I had been to the US before, but I could not understand those classes! The professor's methods were scaring, with all those questionings directed to students, the amount of reading to each class was ridiculous. In addition to that, the reading was incomprehensible. I could read ten times the assigned cases, but when getting to classes it would seem to not have read a line at all.

Judicial opinions, concurrencies, dissents, legal issues, rulings, constitutional principles, justices being called by their names, the levels of appeal... To make things worse, the program I had chosen, a master's degree in Criminal Law, had no international students. I had classes with only Americans, and many of them did not even know I was an international student. To put it simple: it was hard.

After a lot of effort and reading, many straight hours in the law library, academic writing workshops, amazing and helpful professors and great American colleagues, I had finally overcome the difficulties, and I could, at last, enjoy the program I signed to – do not kid yourself, the hard work and the hours spent in the library did not go away.

Years after this experience I am given the opportunity to come up with a legal English manual for law students. I could not be more excited. I spent months brainstorming and taking notes of what were the greatest difficulties experienced by me, and I came up with a book that tries to cover all the important points.

Starting with the legal English language, its understanding is contextualized both in judicial court practices and academic ones. This book brings the necessary information for those who are interested in the American justice system and the practice of law, but also for those who aim to peruse an academic degree in an American law school.

The discussion brought are important and actual, and despite being done in the English language, in the American justice context, they are not limited to that, specially with the current tendency of American criminal policies importations experienced by many countries.

I really hope that this book elucidates the subject, giving confidence to those who wish to challenge themselves in an international experience.

Chapter 1

Comprehending the system and communicating

People who are interested in learning legal English usually have the personal or professional purpose of studying or working abroad (or both). This is the reason why it is interesting to link the study of the legal vocabulary in English with the analysis of a legal system and its structure.

Besides, working with a particular system and its principles and statutes gives us a real background to understand the words, expressions and the grammar used in the legal context, putting away the boring abstractions, making the study more concrete and practical.

In this book, we take the United States (US) Legal System, its regulations and structure under consideration in our analysis. We will also discuss the American legal education, really interesting for those who plan perusing a degree in the US. After that we are going to talk about how the law firms works, entering in the specific law vocabulary ground.

The final topics in this chapter are designated to the communication skills. We will analyze the appropriate verbs to be used in a legal environment, the legal communication through emails and memos, also covering important expression that can be useful when legally speaking or writing.

— 1.1 —
The US Legal System

The US were colonialized by England, and from 1722 on it was decided the English Common Law system would be applied to the colony, in all its 13 states, in consonance with the existing laws, in a way that it was compatible with the local social life. This compatibility provision from the beginning has showed to be inexistent. The common law practice was not appropriate to the colonies, since it was overelaborated, required technical professionals, the judges, and it was absolutely unfamiliar to that population.

The current law was the one arbitrarily applied by magistrates, making, in many occasions, the use of the Bible (David, 2014). With the efforts of fighting the arbitrations and legal uncertainty a codification movement was installed, assuming the written law would bring the security sought.

However, social and economic transformations experienced by the colony in the eighteenth century raised the necessity of a more developed law system, capable of offering protection against absolutism. Suddenly, the common law system seemed to be an option.

With the country's independence from England, it was understood the necessity of a truly American system, independent and adapted to the country's reality. The French Code's system was ventilated as a possibility but the original English model, with its sources and rational, was adopted in all American territory, after all.

It is important to make clear that, since the beginning, the American system presented original characteristics, influenced by Roman law, with many of the original English rules never being applied in that judicial system due to lack of compatibility.

Their similarities, between the US and the English systems, reside in their origin, their implementation, serving the English one as a role model to the American one. But both present many differences, which is inevitable due to different geographic, economic, cultural and political aspects.

The common law tradition, experienced by North America, has developed an adversarial justice system, based on the lawyer's rhetoric, to help create, interpret and also invalidate legal rules during a concrete dispute resolution (Bergman; Goodman; Holm, 2012).

That meaning, the adversarial system is characterized by the parties' engagement, accusation and defense, in a combat or conflict. Only the parties are responsible for presenting evidence to a judge, who assume a passive attitude before the cause. The judge figures as a mere observer, he does not investigate the facts, does not go after evidence of the case, summarizing his activity to making sure the accused individual rights are being respected, such as the observation of evidence rules. It is thus a form of combat, however, its practices are properly regulated. (Bisharat, 2014).

Legal Vocabulary Bank

- **American Common law** – "1. The body of English law that was adopted as the law of the American colonies and supplemented with local enactments and judgments. 2. The body of judge-made law that developed during and after the United States' colonial period, esp. since independence" (Garner, 2016, p. 134).
- **Adversary system** – "A procedural system, such as the Anglo-American legal system, involving active and unhindered parties contesting with each other to put forth a case before an independent decision-maker" (Garner, 2016, p. 21).
- **Evidence** – "Something (including testimony, documents and tangible objects) that tends to prove or disprove, the existence of an alleged fact. 2. The collective mass of things, esp. testimony and exhibits, presented before a tribunal in a given dispute. 3. The body of law regulating the admissibility of what is offered as proof into the record of a legal proceeding" (Garner, 2016, p. 280).

The adversarial system also has as characteristics the orality, being a lawyer-centered procedure, as opposed to the civil law system, in which the procedures are judge-centered. In the first, is the lawyer the one responsible for the theories he decides to explore, which evidence to use, how to examine witnesses as well as how to cross-examine them. These practices result in a speedy and compact trial.

The jury is considered the spine of the American legal system. For that reason, in the next topic, when we study the American legal system in its structure, we will start by the jury trial.

— 1.2 —
The sources of law

Both systems of government in the US, federal and state, share the same major sources of law. In this topic, we will study these main sources of legal rules in the American judicial system.

The four main sources of law in the US justice system are their Constitution, statutes, regulations and case law, in his hierarchical order. The US Constitution is considered the "supreme law of the land", and no inferior law can rule against its "spirit", which is consecrated in its principles, such as the freedom of speech. It is 200 years old and 7 articles and 27 amendments constituting it. It is characterized by its supremacy, but also to its abstraction and equal rights clause.

Every state is subjected to both Constitutions, the US supreme law and the state's constitution – which typically regulates local situations. The Constitution regulates the government actions regarding the citizen's rights. On the other hand, statutory rules regulate individual's actions.

Statutes are sets of written laws, approved through a legislative procedure, such as penal codes and rules of evidence. These rules cannot be conflicting with the Constitution, under the possibility of judicial review by the court that would invalidate unconstitutional laws.

The case law is based on judicial opinions that after deciding on a case are turned into precedent, applicable to future similar cases. The statutory law is stronger than the case law, however it is only valid after it was interpreted and applied to a concrete case. For that reason, it is very common that the case law presents exceptions to statutory and constitutional law, due to judicial interpretation. That is only legal if the ruling resulting from judicial interpretation is constitutional.

Putting in practice, the US Constitution, in its Fourth Amendment, sought to secure the right to privacy inside one's home and personal objects. In order to achieve that, it states:

> The right of the people to be secure in their persons, houses, papers, and effects, against unreasonable searches and seizures, shall not be violated, and no warrants shall issue, but upon probable cause, supported by oath or affirmation, and particularly describing the place to be searched, and the persons or things to be seized (The Constitution..., 2021).

That meaning, to enter somebody's home, to search a person or to have access and/or to seize private documents and otherwise written papers, for example, a warrant should be issued, by a neutral judge, in cases where there is probable cause, identifying specifically its object, place or person.

However, the constitutional **warrant** guarantee, when applied to real cases, generated a great number of exceptions – studied in Constitutional Criminal Procedure classes, under the name of "warrant requirement exceptions". Putting it simple, there are many cases where a warrant can be **waived**. Some examples of these exceptions are: consent, plain view, search incident to arrest, exigent circumstances, automobile exceptions and hot pursuit (Chemerinsky; Levenson, 2018).

For instance, if an officer who is lawfully on the premises finds the evidence of a crime in **plain view**, this evidence seizure or the arrest of the person linked to that evidence is legal, even without a warrant (plain view exception). That is also true when a search is done, without a warrant, in an automobile in which there's **reasonable belief** there are drugs (automobile exception).

All these exceptions come with a long discussion about its terms, such as the reasonable belief definition relating to the automobile exception and the determination of plain view – Does a firefighter, using a leather to reach an electric post, who accidently sees a marijuana plantation in someone's yard over the house's fence, match the plain view requisites? What about the use of drones by the law enforcement?

Moreover, the case law as a source of the law respect the ***stare decisis*** *policy*, that will be discussed by us in a later topic, but, generally speaking, means that the futures cases are bounded to the precedents of the court, even though the policy is not absolute.

Also, as we are going to see, states have great legislative power when it comes to criminal law and procedure rules. For that reason, the criminal law and procedure may vary, depending the state under analysis.

Legal Vocabulary Bank

- **Plain-view doctrine** – "Criminal procedure. The rule permitting a police officer's warrantless seizure and use as evidence of an item seen in plain view from a lawful position or during a legal search when the officer has probable cause to believe that the item is evidence of a crime" (Garner, 2016, p. 571). [Plain view: a place that is easily seen – Merriam Webster Dictionary].
- **Stare decisis** – "The doctrine of precedent, under which a court must follow earlier judicial decisions when the same points arise again in litigation" (Garner, 2016, p. 710).
- **Warrant** – "1. A writ directing or authorizing someone to do an act, esp. one directing law enforcer to make an arrest, a search, or a seizure" (Garner, 2016, p. 820).
- **Warrant clause** – "The clause of the Fourth Amendment to the U.S. Constitution requiring that warrants be issued only on probable cause" (Garner, 2016, p. 821).

- **Waiver** – "The voluntary relinquishment or abandonment – express or implied – of a legal right or advantage; FORFEITURE" (Garner, 2016, p. 817). Ex. Warrant waiver.

— 1.3 —
The US Legal Structure

It is of extreme importance for us to comprehend the rational behind the jury trial, once its rules and principles form the legal thinking in the US. This rational is constituted by two concerns, which are the search for balance between the State and the society powers, as well as the search for fair decisions, based on the jury consensus – twelve people who represent the general population.

The interest behind the practice is the achievement of the juridical truth, instead of a legal one, and for this exact reason there are many rules regarding the evidence that is accepted in court to criminalize and individual, foreclosing the use of both, illegal evidence and involuntary testimonies (Wonsowicz, 2017). The jury proceedings are divided in two parts, the pre-trial phase and the trial phase. In this section, and in all others, we are emphasizing the criminal law and procedure practices, including when discussing the jury proceedings.

— 1.3.1 —
Pre-trial litigation

It takes place before trial, being the moment when the preliminary hearing happens, for example – occasion when the accusation presents evidence that are able to establish, with **probable cause**, that the accused committed the crime at issue. In the state of California, this is a mandatory procedure to all crimes considered **felonies**, that being more serious criminal conducts, which sanctions vary from one year of imprisonment, to life in prison or even the death penalty.

Legal Vocabulary Bank

- **Probable Cause** – "A reasonable ground to suspect that a person has committed or is committing a crime [...] [for jury verdict] under the fourth amendment [...], which amounts to more than a bare suspicion but less than evidence that would justify a conviction [...]" (Garner, 2016, p. 599).
- **Felony** – "A serious crime usually punishable by imprisonment for more than one year or by death" (Garner, 2016, p. 310).

One of the Constitutional principles guarantees that the accused has the right to be judge by his peers, in an impartial manner, that meaning, in a neutral manner, in practice, that means that the selected jurors belong to the same jurisdiction of the accused. Twelve jurors, in a felony case, compose the jury, but that number can be smaller depending on the crime being judged. The jurors are selected from a pull of 60 participants. Some extra jurors are selected, figuring as substitutes, in case a replacement is needed during trial.

During the jury selection, the volunteers are questioned, through a process called *voir dire*, which takes place in order to certify the candidate belongs to the accused's jurisdiction, speaks fluent English, also working as a tool to questions the candidate's tendencies or inclinations – **bias**.

During jury selection, each part has the right to refuse jurors, excluding them from the proceeding. This refusal of the candidate can happen due to explicit reason, being justified by the part, also known as **for cause challenges**.

In the other hand, the exclusion of a candidate might take place without justification needed, simply because the part wishes so, also known as **peremptory challenges**. This situation can occur in a limited number – in California, it is possible to have 10 peremptory challenges and 25 if the case involves the death penalty (Bisharat, 2014).

> **Legal Vocabulary Bank**
>
> - **Bias** – "Inclination; prejudice; predilection. – bias, *vb.* – biased, *adj.*" (Garner, 2016, p. 74).
> - **For cause** – "For a legal reason or ground. * The phrase expresses a common standard governing the removal of a civil servant or an employee under contract – for-cause, *adj.*" (Garner, 2016, 2011, p. 316).
> - **Peremptory** – "1. Final; absolute; conclusive; incontrovertible <the king's peremptory order>. 2. Not requiring any shown cause; arbitrary <peremptory challenges>. *adj.*" (Garner, 2016, p. 564)

As we can notice, the jury proceedings can be long and tiring, lasting for weeks or even months, depending on how complex the case at issue is. Only after the jury selection the trial takes place.

— 1.3.2 —
Trial litigation

A jury must observe important constitutional principles, such as the presumption of innocence, wich makes the burden of proof fall under the accusation responsibility. The evidence criteria is that it must prove "**beyond a reasonable doubt**" what is being stated.

The privilege against self-incrimination is also valid, and the accused has the right to remain silent. Also, **character evidence**, regarding the accused, used in his disadvantage are also prohibited. The illegally obtained evidence ate inadmissible under the **exclusionary rule**, which also does not admit **hearsay** as evidence (Wonsowicz, 2017).

Besides that, the adversarial system is characterized in an expressive manner through the confrontation clause, which guarantees the presence of the accused to hear the witnesses, in addition to the right to **cross-examination.** Finally, when the crime discussed is punished with prison time, the accused has the right to a defense council (Bisharat, 2014).

Legal Vocabulary Bank

- **Beyond a reasonable doubt** – "is the standard used by a jury to determine weather a criminal defendant is guilty [...]. In deciding weather guilt has been proved beyond a reasonable doubt, the jury must begin with the presumption that the defendant is innocent" (Garner, 2016, p. 625).
- **Character evidence** – "Evidence regarding someone's general personality traits or propensities, of a praiseworthy or blameworthy nature; evidence of a person's moral standing in a community" (Garner, 2016, p. 289).

- **Exclusionary rule** – "1. Evidence. Any rule that excludes or suppresses evidence <despite many exceptions, hearsay has long been inadmissible under an exclusionary rule. 2. Criminal procedure. A rule that excludes or suppresses evidence obtained in violation of an accused person's constitutional rights [...]" (Garner, 2016, p. 287).
- **Hearsay** – "Traditionally, testimony that is given by a witness who relates not what he or she knows personally, but what others have said, and that is therefore dependent on the credibility of someone other than the witness. Such testimony is generally inadmissible under the rules of evidence" (Garner, 2016, p. 352).
- **Cross-examination** – "The questioning of a witness at a trial or hearing by the party opposed to the party who called the witness to testify. * The purpose of cross-examination is to discredit a witness before the fact-finder in any of several ways, as by bringing out contradictions and improbabilities in early testimony, by suggesting doubts to the witness, and by trapping the witness into admissions that weaken the testimony. [...]" (Garner, 2016, p. 191).

Just as the jury selection and the pre-trial phase as a whole, the trial can be time-consuming, also lasting up to months. In addition to that, it is a high costly proceeding, institutionally and as to the social sources.

There are costs relating to the structure maintained by the State – court rooms, personnel, accusations and defense lawyers – it is estimated that 75% of the criminal cases in California are defended by a public defender, nominated by the court, thus, paid by the State (Bisharat, 2014).

Also important to emphasize that the jurors find their personal and professional life compromised by jury services. Studies show that after California adopted a 8 jurors trial, instead of the original 12, in cases regarding **misdemeanors**, millions of dollars were saved in benefit of the State a year, that without taking into account the costs regarding the privet employers (Bisharat, 2014). Finally, jury trials are grounded by their high emotional costs, to all parties involved in the proceedings.

As we are going to see, the American states hold great legislative power. For this reason administrative and judicial organization may vary according to the specific region under analysis. Nevertheless, a federal and a state sphere constitute the judicial system in the country.

In the state sphere, as a general rule, there are District Courts, formed by hundreds of judges and **officers of the courts**. As a second level of appeal, there is the Court of Appeals, which, in the California state, are in the number of six "Appellate Courts" – from the first to the sixth district. These courts are categorized in divisions.

The cases are decided, in the corresponding division, by three **justices**, whose **opinions** may be subjected to publishing, in state reports, as long as some criteria are filled, such as the establishment of a new ruling, a decisions on legal issues regarding public interest, critics regarding existing legal rules or significant contribution to the legal literature (California Constitution, art. VI, § 14; Cal. Rules of Court, rule 8.1105(c)).

Therefore, when one of the parties disagree with the decision emanated from the District Courts, it is possible to appeal. In first instance Courts there is testimony examination and evidence appreciation by a judge or jury. In a second level of appeal the Court does not reevaluate testimonies or physical evidence, restricting the analysis to the case file, in order to certify the law was properly applied, as well as the proceedings regarding the case at issue.

As a general rule, the decisions made by the courts of appeal are final, and the reason for that is because the State Supreme Court (third level of appeal) only appreciates cases where some law conflict is present.

The lawyers take part in the justices' decision making by presenting written memos and carrying out oral argumentations. The decision does not have to be unanimous, being admitted **dissenting opinions** among justices. A very interesting fact is that, in California, the appeal must be appreciated in up to 90 days after the case was submitted. Otherwise, the justices' salaries might be retained, according to stated in the California Constitution.

The State Supreme Court has the authority to review the Appellate Court's decisions, being able to decide about important legal issues, maintaining law uniformity. There is one particularity that must be pointed out. In cases involving the death penalty, the appeal is directed to the State Supreme Court directly, not going through the Appellate Court.

A Chief Justice and six Associate Justices are nominated by the State Governor to assemble the State Supreme Court. The nomination has to be confirmed by the public during the voting procedures. Justices work for a 12 years term, being able to be reelected.

In California, three women, one of them being the Chefe Justice (Tani Gorre Cantil-Sakauye), and four men form the Supreme Court. It is based in San Francisco (holding sessions in January, March, May, September and October, during the year of 2020), Los Angeles (sessions being held in April, June and December of the same period), and in Sacramento (sessions in February and November of 2020). The Oral Argument Calendar is available at the Court's webpage.

Legal Vocabulary Bank

- **Misdemeanor** – "A crime that is less serious than a felony, and is usu. Punishable by fine, penalty, forfeiture, or confinement (usu. for a brief term) in a place other than prison (such as a county jail)" (Garner, 2016, p. 488).
- **Officer of the Court** – "A person who is charged with upholding the law and administering the judicial system. Typically, officer of the court refers to a judge, clerk, bailiff, sheriff or

the like, but the term also applies to a lawyer, who is obliged to obey court rules and who owes a duty of candor to the court" (Garner, 2016, p. 537).
- **Justice** – "2. A judge, esp. of an appellate court or a court of last resort. – Abbreviation J. (and. In plural, JJ.)" (Garner, 2016, p. 426).
- **Opinion** – "1. A court's written statement explaining its decision in a given case, usu. including the statement of facts, points of law, rational and dicta. – Abbr. op." (Garner, 2016, p. 541).
- **Dissenting Opinion** – "An opinion by one or more judges who disagree with the decision reached by the majority" (Garner, 2016, p. 541).
- **Concurrence** – "1. Agreement; assent. 2. A vote cast by a judge in favor of the judgment reached, often on grounds differing from those expressed in the opinion or opinions explaining the judgment. 3. A separate written opinion explaining such a vote" (Garner, 2016, p. 142).
- **Legal Opinion** – "A written document in which an attorney provides his or her understanding of the law as applied to assumed facts" (Garner, 2016, p. 542).

As to the federal level, its legal authority is related to cases involving the law's constitutionality, cases in which ambassadors or ministers compose one of the parts, or where there are state disputes. There are some subjects that can only be appreciated in the federal level, such as the maritime law and bankruptcy, existing, in the last case, specialized courts for the matter.

In order to make it clearer, the system encompasses 94 District Courts, at least one in each state, 13 Courts of Appeal, as a second instance, and, finally, in the highest hierarchic level, there is the American Supreme Court – composed by 9 justices, who are nominated by the president of the United States, nomination to be confirmed by the Senate.

The Supreme Court work calendar is established in terms, that last one year, being the justices' activities differentiated between "sitting" and "recess". During the "sitting" period, that comprises two weeks a month, the justices hear cases and give opinions. During the other period, known as "recess" (during the other two weeks of the month), they write their opinions[1].

The majority of cases that reach the Supreme Court and are in fact, submitted to the Court's exam, regard the revision of lower court's decisions, what implicates in the absence of a jury, with no witnesses being heard. What is actually considered by the justices are the files, accompanied by written memos – briefs – elaborated by lawyers, with their arguments on the case.

During plenary review, lawyers are allowed to oral argumentation for 30 minutes. However, only few of the cases directed to the Court are actually admitted and examined. Each year 8 thousand cases are filed in the Court, but only to 80 of them

---

1   For more information, go to: <supremecourt.gov>.

are granted plenary review. The Court, without plenary review, disposes other 100 cases.

There is no compulsory analysis of the cases filed; therefore, the Court chooses what will be subjected to examination by the justices under some criteria. The case must be relevant, nationally speaking, it must bring lower court's decisions harmonization – when conflict is present – and must be precedent valuable. The majority of votes form the Supreme Court's decision – unanimity is not necessary.

These are the main points regarding the American Justice system and structure. We will come back to many of the issues here discussed in future analysis made in this book.

— 1.4 —
The US Legal Education and Law School Life

As stated before, the Legal English interest comes along with the intention of studying abroad. After the student or professional has decided he or she wants to pursue an international degree, a journey takes place in the academic's life. Choosing the schools to apply for, studying for the language proficiency test, gathering all the documents and recommendation letter's needed and writing essays are part of the activities that will take all the candidate's free time.

Once the student is approved to a law program abroad, a whole new range of insecurities is introduced to his life. To start, a very common preoccupation among foreign students is the legal English. "Will I be able to attend classes, participate, take tests and pass them? Is my English good enough? Can I manage to write a thesis or any other type of independent research project?" The typical international student has an ESL (English as a Second Language) degree, lacking the professional or academic legal English knowledge.

As a matter of fact, the legal vocabulary for first year students of law are difficult even in their first languages what to say in a second language? But the legal vocabulary is not the only trouble to be faced by international students. The international legal education, with its specific methodology, is also something that requires adaptation.

Once as an international student myself, I took the liberty to, in this title, to share some of my experiences in an American Law School. A few chapters ahead we will dedicate ourselves to the analysis of the case method itself, used both, in the American law schools and in the practice of law under the common law system. Here I intend to share impressions about the college life, class methods, professors and other singularities of the American culture.

Students who wish to become lawyers, after finishing high school, must go through four years of undergraduate school. After that they must apply and be accepted to a law school, for a three-year program. The admission process is complex, with a curriculum analysis, recommendation letters examination, among others. But, in addition to all of that, the student who wants to get into a law school must pass a test called LSAT (Law School Admission Test). According to the test website, the evaluation "is designed specifically to assess critical reading, analytical reasoning, logical reasoning, and persuasive writing skills" (LSAC, 2021).

Once the student is accepted, and classes start, he becomes a 1L (first year of Law student), followed by 2Ls and 3Ls – these last ones, soon to be lawyers. However, graduating in law school does not make you an attorney in the US. After the graduation – what grants the academic a degree of Juris Doctor (J.D.), students must take, and pass, the Bar Exam, in the state they intend to practice law, to become lawyers.

For those who are already graduated in Law, the Law Schools offer graduate programs, such as the Masters of Law (L.LM) – that can be professional or academic, – or even a Ph.D. These programs are also offered for international students that hold a law degree in their country.

In 2014 I was accepted at University of California – Los Angeles (UCLA) as a Masters of Law graduate student (an academic LLM). The program is designed to last one academic year, with full-time classes, from Mondays to Fridays. A typical day in a law student's life resumes to being in the law school for the whole day – when not in classes, the students are studding and reading in the law library or experiencing the campus life, that relies on a variety of extracurricular activities, courses, study groups, community centers, gyms, sports courts, cafeterias, restaurants, among others.

The schools inside the campus organize lectures and debates, with important guests, routinely, usually making use of the lunch breaks, serving lunch for those enrolled to participate – sandwiches and burritos, accompanied with potato chips and soda are very popular. Students can also work in the campus' stores, libraries, sports' centers or other administrative departments, during flexible hours.

The reason most students choose to stay in campus for full-time periods is related to the huge amount of reading that is imposed every day, due to the Socratic method, in practice in the American Law Schools.

The method, named after its inventor, Socrates, consists in the questioning of the students, by the professor, until a contradiction is exposed. It is used in law schools as a tool to promote discussions among a large group of students. The professor is the mediator, using probing questions, until the real issue of a subject rises. But in order for that to work, the student must get to classes prepared, with all the material assigned read, what takes us to another particularity of the legal education method in the US.

In a common law system, based on precedents, the study of law is, in great part, done through the case study. So, if we are discussing, in a constitutional criminal procedure class, the

Fourth Amendment right to warrant exceptions, lets' say, the plain view exception, the students, before class, must read and brief all the assigned cases on the matter, so they are ready to discuss them during the meeting, through the professor's mediation, done by questioning the students, repeatedly. Not being able to answer the professor in class, because one is not prepared, since he or she has not read the material, can be a problem – there are statements of situations where the professor has asked the unprepared student to leave the class.

As stated by the University of Chicago Law School (2021), "the Socratic Method is not used at UChicago to intimidate, nor to "break down" new law students, but instead for the very reason Socrates developed it: to develop critical thinking skills in students and enable them to approach the law as intellectuals" We are going to discuss the particularities of the case method and the practice of briefing cases ahead.

The law school, at least at UCLA, has a very nice environment. Classrooms are modern and spacious, professors, besides being experts in their fields, are helpful and welcoming – they have what is called *office ours*, a period during a day or two of the week when they are available for students in their offices, outside class, to talk, solve doubts and give academic or professional advises. Many professors also take groups of students to have lunch in the faculty center, as an opportunity to talk outside the class.

An interesting UCLA "law school" extra-curricular activity is called "Bar Review", making a joke with the Bar exam. Every week, one bar in Los Angles is chosen, so students can go, have drinks and give a review of the venue. Of course, that is just an excuse for law students to party.

Talking about parties, fraternities are very common on campus, as shown in the movies. But they are not the only housing options. The University has many housing possibilities, such as dorms for singles students, small apartments for those who like to share, and even family houses for those who have kids.

In Los Angeles, Westwood, the neighborhood where the UCLA campus is located, offers a lot of small apartment options for rent, even though prices are not compelling – it is one of the most expensive areas in town.

I have pursued a graduate degree in criminal law, so all the credits I took during the Masters' program were criminal law and procedure related. But the options are many, such as Business Law, International and Comparative Law, Media, Entertainment, and Technology Law and Policy Specialization, or Public Interest Law (UCLA, 2021).

Besides meeting international students from all over the world, living abroad can be a very enriching experience. Getting to know a different culture, explore a completely new city, make small group trips and new good friends are all great opportunities when you move to a different country, to experience a student life. In the case of LA, the days at Santa Monica beach are simple remarkable.

The city is very cultural, with a lot of museums, exhibitions, shows, and home of the LA Philharmonic. On Fridays there are free jazz concerts on LACMA's museum backyard, where people have picnics, drinking wine. The California state holds many great attractions, besides its beautiful beaches, such as the Yosemite National Park, the Napa Valley with its vineyards, and Lake Tahoe, for those who like winter sports. Even a Disneyland park is available! If you ever have the chance to study abroad, it is a life changing experience.

Image 1.1 – UCLA Campus

— 1.5 —
Law firms structure and practice areas

In the US, a law firm structure can vary, depending on factors such as the size of the firm and its complexity. The most common structure includes the managing partners, shareholders, associates, "off counsel" attorneys, summer associates and staff.

The managing partners are senior level lawyers or the ones who have founded the firm. They are usually compromised to the firm's strategies and employee culture, handling executive meetings. Despite that, it is very common for managing partners to practice the law in a full-time mode.

Below the managing partners, who come first in the firm's hierarchy, there are the law firm partners. They are usually shareholders, but the partnership may also vary, depending on the firm.

The younger lawyers are usually hired as associates (junior or senior), and maybe one day they might become partners, depending on the results the professional brings to the firm and his experience. The process of becoming a partner may take from six to nine years.

The "Of Counsel" role is served to those who don't work directly for the firm, celebrating independent contracts for specific cases. "Most of-counsel lawyers work on a part-time basis, manage their own cases, and supervise associates and staff" (The Balance Careers, 2021).

Summer associates are law school students, who work as interns during the summer vacation. This can be an unpaid or a paid internship. The summer internship can be a powerful tool in guarantying a hired position in the law firm after graduation.

Other professionals, besides lawyers, also make part of a law firm's team. Administrative workers, such as secretaries, and paralegals are usually in the firm's structure.

Paralegals are professionals who provide support to attorneys. Their responsibilities usually encompass legal precedent research, legal documents' preparation, also being responsible for the investigative work on cases. Some law schools offer paralegal certificate's program (ParalegalEdu.org, 2021).

The law fields are also present in that system in a great number. Corporate law deals with commercial legal transactions, advising corporations, with a less adversarial practice, just as patent lawyers, who represent clients who wish to obtain patents. The Criminal defense field is characterized by a highly adversarial practice with trial performance. The attorneys can be private practitioners or public defenders.

Government attorneys interpret and enforce the law, working directly for the State. In addition to those practice areas there are tax attorneys, family attorneys, labor law attorneys, immigrations practitioners, among others.

— 1.6 —
Persons and documents in Court

In this topic we bring important actors in the American justice system, more specifically the parts they play in Court, as well as some documents that are usually present in the daily law practice.

It is simpler to imagine the role played by the judge and the attorneys in a courtroom. However, other court officers play an important part in the justice administration, and their names in English are usually unknown. Also, the parts of the case are designated differently, depending on the nature of the case, if criminal or civil, for example.

The courtroom works with the presence of a judge and the attorneys, as mentioned before, but also with the activity of clerks, a bailiff, witnesses, and the parties. A clerk is a public official, whose activities may be exercised by law students, recently graduates or even lawyers, who are responsible in assisting the judge with his decisions' research and writing, also being useful to manage the cases under the judge's responsibility.

The bailiff is an officer of the court responsible for maintaining the order while proceedings take place. As to the witnesses, common sense knowledge is that, after being called to testify in court, they give testimony under oath. However, there are many witnesses' types, such as a character witness, alibi witness, lay or expert witness, rebuttal or corroborating witness, among others.

A character witness is the one who testifies about someone's character and reputation. Usually, this kind of testimony is only aloud in court when it benefits the accused. An alibi witness testifies about where the defendant was, other than the place where the crime happened, supporting the accused's defense.

A lay witness presents no expertise, simply giving an opinion or making an inference in her testimony, as opposed to an expert testimony, made by an expert witness, which contains a degree of knowledge in a particular subject – expert witnesses can be doctors, engineers, accountants, among many others. A corroborating testimony confirms someone else's and a rebuttal witness contradicts, or tries to, the evidence presented. (For more see The Black Law's Dictionary, "witness".)

As to the parties, their designation depends on the nature of the cause. But the person who is being sued in a civil case or is being accused in a criminal one – the one who is in the passive pole of the action – is the defendant. On the other side, the one who brings the civil suit against a defendant is the plaintiff (active party). The party responsible to charge de offender and move a penal action against him is the accusation, usually composed by the prosecutor's office – the prosecutor represent the government in criminal proceedings. In the second level of appeal, the party who takes action, asking for a decision review, is called petitioner or appellant.

Finally, it is important to understand the concept behind the "reasonably prudent person", rational, very used in trials to establish culpability. It regards a hypothetical person, used theoretically to construct arguments in court, as a reference. In Brazil, we use the same concept under the idea of "homem médio": "Such a person's actions are the guide in determining whether an individual's actions were reasonable" (Krois-Lindner, 2009, p. 11).

Legal Vocabulary Bank

- **Reasonable person** – "A hypothetical use as a legal standard, esp. to determine weather someone acted with negligence; espec., a person who exercises the degree of attention, knowledge, intelligence, and judgment that society requires of its members for the protection of their own and of other's interests. * The reasonable persons acts sensibly, does things without serious delay, and takes proper but not excessive precautions" (Garner, 2016, p. 626).

Image 1.2 – Persons in court

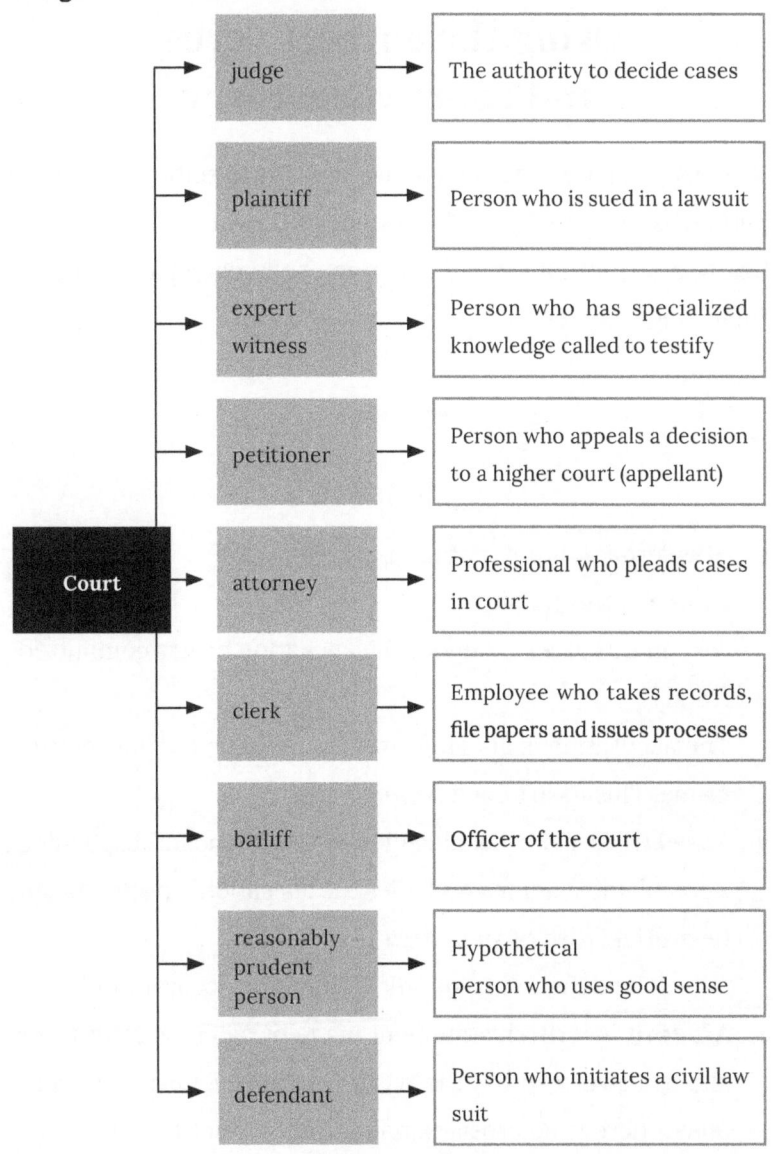

Court		
→	judge	The authority to decide cases
→	plaintiff	Person who is sued in a lawsuit
→	expert witness	Person who has specialized knowledge called to testify
→	petitioner	Person who appeals a decision to a higher court (appellant)
→	attorney	Professional who pleads cases in court
→	clerk	Employee who takes records, file papers and issues processes
→	bailiff	Officer of the court
→	reasonably prudent person	Hypothetical person who uses good sense
→	defendant	Person who initiates a civil law suit

Source: Based on Cambridge's International Legal English course, Unit 1 – The practice of law, Persons in court diagram, p. 11.

— 1.7 —
Using the correct verbs and court vocabulary

The legal activity requires the use of some specific vocabulary and verbs. We have highlighted some of these important words below, also putting some of them in use in examples, to make their usage clearer.

In practice

- **Allegation**: It is a hypothesis, stated as true, a fact asserted by one of the parties.
  "Joseph was arrested under the allegation he has committed fraud."
  The accusation is alleging, as a fact, Joseph committed the crime. This hasn't been proved yet.
- **Answer**: The main pleading filed by the defendant responding a complaint. It admits or denies the allegation. An answer can be *drafted, filed* or *submitted*.
  "The defendant, in his answer, denied the accusations."
- **Affidavit**: A written statement made by a person after he or she has sworn to tell the truth, which is voluntarily made. Since there is no cross-examination, it is not the same as a deposition.
  "An affidavit was *filed/submitted* by the prosecution."

- **Acquittal**: A decision that discharge or absolves the accused, finding him not guilty.
  "Joseph, after tried for the crime of fraud, has been acquitted."
- **Bench trial**: A trial that happens without a jury, before a single judge. The decision emanates from him, regarding both the facts and the law.
- **Brief**: Document with a detailed court case, a summary of important points. Students do it with legal opinions as part of their academic activities in the Case Method. Attorneys do it for the parties or to help the judge in his decision-making.
- **Chambers**: The judge's office.
- **Charge**: The act of accusing someone of committing an offense.
  "Joseph was charged with fraud."
- **Complaint**: The first plead filed by a plaintiff in a civil case or the first document that sets forth the basis for an offense charge; also a notice to the defendant that a legal action is in place. The complaint can be *drafted, filed, served* or *submitted*.
  "The complaint was filed out electronically, after the plaintiff had his car crashed by the defendant."
- **Conviction**: A guilty criminal sentence.
- **Deposition**: A testimony given by a witness out of the court. It is usually reduced in written to later use.
  "A deposition was made by the storeowner, who saw the defendant stabbing the victim."

- **Discovery**: A pre-trial phase of a proceeding when the parties gather information on their cases through depositions and interrogatories.
- **Indictment**: Document related to the formal accusation of a crime. Only after that the prosecution of the accused can begging. It is usually made by a grad jury.
"The accused was indicted of selling illegal drugs."
- **Injunction**: Legal order demanding or prohibiting an act by someone. An injunction can be *issued* or *served*.
"An injunction was issued to the witness prohibiting her to leave the town."
- **Impeachment**: Consists in discrediting a witness testimony or any other evidence. If a witness is caught lying she can be impeached.
- **Motion**: An application to a court to obtain an order, ruling or decision. There is, for example, motion to suppress evidence that were illegally obtained, so the other party cannot use them in court. A motion can be *drafted*, *submitted* or *filed*.
- **Mistrial**: When a trial is not valid we have a mistrial. In that case, a new trial must take place. A cause of mistrial is de admissibility in court of an illegal obtained evidence, for example, which can lead to the need of a new trial.
- **Oath**: A formal declaration, usually sworn to God, that the person is saying the truth.
- **Objection**: An opposition to what is being said or what is happening in court. The reasons to object are learned by law students in Evidence classes.

- **Pleading**: Written statement requesting the court to act, exerting its judicial power – setting forth the cause of action or the defense in a case. A plead can be *drafted, filed, served* or *submitted*.
- **Subpoena**: An official order demanding the presentation of the person in court, under penalty. A subpoena can be *issued* or *filed*.
- **Take the stand**: To take the witness position in court, to share information and expertise as a witness.
- **Writ**: An instruction document to someone to be involved in a legal process.

Source: Garner, 2016.

As you can see in some of these sentences, there are verbs best suited to refer to actions related to court documents. To give an example we wrote that a motion could be *drafted, submitted* or *filed*. Understanding the meaning of these verbs and comprehending the difference between them will facilitate their correct use.

To draft means to make a first version of a document, that may be changed later; it is a start point of an idea, that will be developed, better organized in a final version of a document. **To issue** relates to release something official; to send something (an information, an order or others) directly to a specific person. **To file** is to record, to present, to register officially. **To serve**

means to deliver a legal document and **to submit,** to deliver formally a document.

Also, there are some important verbs relating to what the law says, which use is really recommended in a legal environment. To mention a few important verbs, we can say that the law *provides* information, *specifies* prohibited conducts, *lays down* conditions, *states* maximum prices, *determines* the information needs, *imposes* sanctions, prescribes conducts, *sets forth* rights, *estipulate* requirements, *provides* examples.

In practice

- "**The statute *provides* that** no person shall receive a certificate permitting him to work in a coal mine in this State unless he shall have had two years' practical experience as a miner or with a miner [...]." (Bulletin of the Bureau of Labor, 1911, p. 316)
- "The Art. 4(2) of **the Statute *stipulates* that** the Court may exercise its functions and powers on the territory of any State Party [...]" The Rome Statute.
- **The statute *lays down*** what the applicable rule is.

The idea is absolutely not investing in a high legalistic stile – what should actually be avoided, as we are going to see in future topics, but to use the correct verb in order to match the action to be taken with determined legal document.

Miscommunication can be a big problem in an attorney's life, as a matter a fact, to anyone's life, but in the legal practice, both writing and speaking skills are very important work tools.

— 1.8 —
Communicating

Since communicating well is a basic skill to any lawyer, at any part of the globe, the correct grammar as well as the written rules must be followed. However, professional e-mails and memos have a specific structure that differs from those messages sent to friends and family. In this topic we are going to work with the structures of these professional communication tools.

When writing an e-mail or a memo to a client, a co-worker or a partner, for example, the main topics on any messages are, in this order, the greetings, a reference to a previous contact, the purpose of the present contact, a closure and, if it is the case, the express of the interest in future contact with that person.

The greeting part involves directing the message to a specific person, using the correct treatment pronoun (Dear Mr./Mrs., for example), saying "hello" in a more formal manner ("I hope this message finds you well" is very much used). After that, it is highly recommended the writer refer to a previous contact (made by phone, personally or even through a previous e-mail) when it is the case, before making clear the purpose of the present contact.

If no previous contact has ever taken place, the next step after the greeting part is making clear why you are contacting the person. This has to be polite, but clear and objective. In the closing part is really important to make yourself available for solving remaining doubts or moving forward on the conversation, depending on the case. Finally, expressing interest in future contacts, when that is actually interesting for the writer or caller, is a very polite way to end.

In practice

- **Greeting**
  - "Dear [family name]" – Dear Mrs. Thompsom;
  - "To whom it may concern" – when you don't know the name of the person you are writing to.
- **Referring to previous contact**
  - "In response to your previous contact..."
  - "Further to our telephone conversation..."
  - "Thank you for your e-mail...."
  - "As mentioned by Susan, you had previously demonstrated to he an interest in...."
- **Making clear the purpose**
  - "I am writing to inform..."
  - "The reason why I am calling is..."
  - "The purpose of my contact is..."

- **Closing – offering further assistance**
  - "Do not hesitate to contact me should you have any further questions..."
- **Expressing interest in future contact**
  - "I look forward to hearing from you/to meeting you..."

Follow up e-mails and phone calls are common practice in the professional American culture. This is the opportunity to inform or ask about the progress of a situation/case or to get feedbacks on any issue. It is also a good strategy to reestablish contact with and to be remembered by clients.

— 1.9 —
Important advise, explanation and negotiation expressions

Lawyers are also required to give opinion on legal matters, among other situations. Having a clear communication is really important to avoid confusions, misinterpretation of the situation and the complications that can come from it. There are some phrases that signalize what is being said is, in fact, an opinion.

In less formal situations opinions are given using expressions such as "I believe...", "In my opinion..." and "I would say...". Adding to them adverbs of manner such as *really, strongly, truly* and *honestly*, can strengthen these expressions. "I strongly believe..." and "I really think...", for example.

In a legal environment, sometimes, the expressions used to give opinion may need to be more formal. Some good options are:

- "I would argue that..."
- "From my perspective.
- "As far as I'm concerned..."
- "It seems to me that..."
- "The way I see it..."
- "If you ask me..."

In practice

- A prospective client telephones to your office, saying he wants to get married, but, since this is his second marriage and he already has two daughters, he is worried about his patrimony, once he wants to make sure his daughters have conditions to go college and have a confortable life.
  You, as a lawyer, would probably advise him to get a prenuptial agreement, offering your services to do that. A prenuptial agreement is a contract, celebrated before marriage by a couple, which gives them control over some legal rights, specially regarding to what happens if they get divorced – as how they are sharing their patrimony.

> You could express your opinion by saying: "**The way I see it**, in you case a prenup. is highly recommended" or "**If you ask me**, I would advise you to get a prenup".

For advising clients, more as a recommendation to what they should do in specific situations, the lawyer can also use expressions such as "I recommend", "I would advise you", "I suggest that" or, " Another way of... would be".

- "**I recommend that** you stop making contact with this person."
- "**I would advise you to** keep all the receipts regarding the services hired...."
- "**I suggest that** you refuse signing the contract..."
- "**One other way of** solving the problem **would be to** contact the landlord..."

Finally, it is important to the legal daily practice to manage negotiation expressions. Being familiar with common phrases may be helpful to face-to-face negotiating sessions, as well as to written informal communications. The professional can make use of some of the following sentences:

- "I'm afraid that's out of the question..."
- "We suggest..."
- "That would be not possible for us..."
- "We would like..."
- "I think we could leave with that..."

In practice

- Negotiating is more present than ever in the American justice system. Even in the penal sphere, with the plea-bargaining, more than 95% of criminal cases are solved through negotiation.

  Let's imagine you are a civil attorney and your client is getting divorced. There is no prenuptial agreement and during a meeting in you office you have to help, joined by the other's party attorney, deciding the ex-couple's division of property. You, representing the interests of you client, have to express that what the other party is offering is not good enough, and that you cannot accept the deal in this terms. You can say that using expressions like: *"That would not be possible for us. We suggest that..."* or *"I'm afraid that is out of the question, my client is not willing to sell the house"*.

Finally, we would like to bring some expressions used to explain your thoughts and ideas, or make a situation clear. *That is, Allow me to explain, Means that, Put simply, In other words,* are helpful expressions when explaining something to someone.

In Practice

- "Driving under the influence is against the law. *That is*, you cannot drink and drive. *Allow me to explain*, if you drink and drive and a police officer stops you, you can go to jail. *In other words*, you become a criminal. *Put simply*, when you drink, get a Uber."

We have also come up with an e-mail draft, as an example of the writing communication skills we have covered in this chapter.

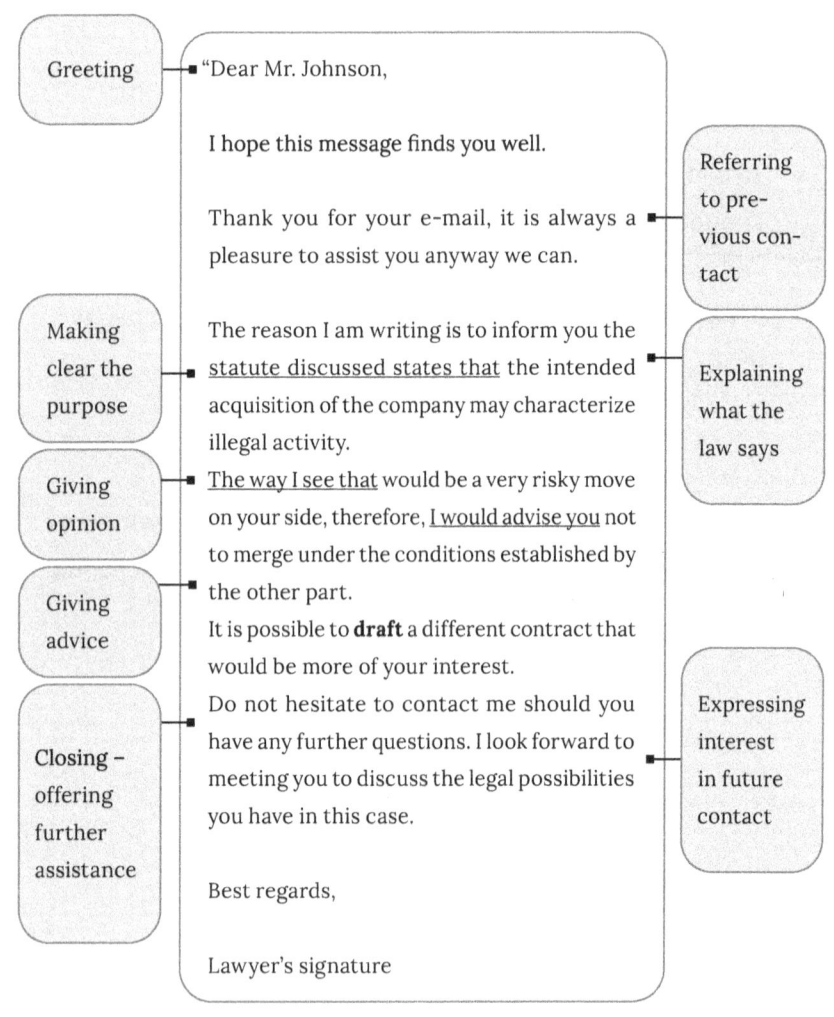

Greeting	"Dear Mr. Johnson,
	I hope this message finds you well.
Referring to previous contact	Thank you for your e-mail, it is always a pleasure to assist you anyway we can.
Making clear the purpose	The reason I am writing is to inform you the <u>statute discussed states that</u> the intended acquisition of the company may characterize illegal activity.
Explaining what the law says	
Giving opinion	<u>The way I see that</u> would be a very risky move on your side, therefore, <u>I would advise you</u> not to merge under the conditions established by the other part.
Giving advice	It is possible to **draft** a different contract that would be more of your interest.
Closing – offering further assistance	Do not hesitate to contact me should you have any further questions. I look forward to meeting you to discuss the legal possibilities you have in this case.
Expressing interest in future contact	
	Best regards,
	Lawyer's signature

In this chapter we got in touch with the first aspects of the Legal English and the American justice system. We have started by analyzing the American justice system, taking under consideration the jury system, which is the heart of America's legal democracy.

As to the legal structure in the country, we have covered its state and federal sphere, regarding all levels of appeal, emphasizing important vocabulary related to the Court and the law practice.

Finally, we have covered Legal English grammar and structure regarding communication skills, also worrying in demonstrate the use of important verbs and expressions in the attorney's daily practice.

Chapter 2

Working with the case method

As stated before, the common law systems, as well as the legal education in countries where the common law is applied, have as a method the precedents and the case study. The legal rules are valid only after they have been applied to a concrete case, which becomes a reference on the matter, being used as a source of the law to all similar cases to come.

In this topic we are studying this methodology and how does it shape the American legal system, also discussing about case briefing, legal issues identification, argument strategies and sources of law.

— 2.1 —
The case method

"casebook method. (1915) An inductive system of teaching law in which students study specific cases, designed as a teaching aid." (Garner, 2016, p. 99)

As mentioned before, to prepare for classes, law students read and brief legal cases, in order to identify what ruling comes out of it and how and why it is applied to further situations. The class is conducted by the professor, who asks questions about the cases assigned, such as the facts involving the case, the case issue and the judges' opinions, to elucidate the law applied and how did the magistrates get to that conclusion.

The analysis of the law at issue is contextualized, with a lot of real examples, which may lead to better retention on the matter on the long-term. The students are responsible for finding the answers for the questions, what, consequently, prepare them to the law practice, which consists mostly in researching and finding answers. That activity benefits from the court judges' opinions on cases, since they usually develop innumerous argumentative pages before reaching a legal principle.

In addition to all that, the critical thinking is a great benefit from the method, since students analyze the cases and the questions, sharing different points of view in class, what gives them a different perspective of the problem discussed. The cases studied are the ones decided on levels of appeal, which decision is given by three judges (in the case of State Courts of Appeal), whose opinions can be unanimous, or may contemplate dissenting or concurring opinions. As stated before, the majority of opinions are taken under consideration when deciding a case.

> Judicial opinions (also known as legal opinions, legal decisions, or cases) are written decisions authored by judges explaining how they resolved a particular legal dispute and explaining their reasoning. An opinion tells the story of the case: what the case is about, how the court is resolving the case, and why [...]." (Kerr, 2005, p. 1)

But if we should summarize, the case method is used to teach legal analysis, which consists in a "process of distilling discrete legal issues from stories and developing arguments to support the resolution of those legal issues" (Bergman, 2012, p. xi).

We can call legal analysis the process of imposing legal meaning to stories and there are two main tasks when legally analyzing an issue: to identify the controversial(s) legal issue(s) and to develop arguments.

The legal issues are pointed by the appellants or the **respondents,** or by both, in the context of the appeal, regarding the issues they want the court to review in their favor. The legal issues may be singular or multiple – which makes the analysis much more complex – and that is the reason why this kind of cases are the favorite ones to appear in a law school final exam. Examples of legal issues may encompass jury misinstruction or weather the police had the right to search without a warrant, also covering law vocabulary definitions in determined statute, such as the definition of the word *night* or *dwelling*, among others.

The activity of argument developing, also called *legal rhetoric*, is the toll lawyers have at their disposal to convince the court of their thesis, making judges decide in their favor. The arguments go into two directions, to convince the judges on their position, and to invalidate the other party positions. We are deepening this subject analysis when we talk about argumentation strategy (Bergman, 2012, p. 2).

Legal analyses must be faced as a process where there are competing arguments rather than a single conclusion. The goal is the appropriate application, through the argumentation process, of an abstract principle to a concrete scenario – which is needed due to the principle's indeterminacy, necessary for its widely application. But interpretation is not always necessary. It is waved in cases where there is prior judicial opinion which can solve the question or when, for the resolution of the matter, there are determinate rules.

A judge, when expressing his opinion on a decision (**holding**), gives arguments, which are originated by lawyers' rhetoric, having been submitted in the lawyer's case brief. Despite all the positive points regarding the method, there are critics to it, such as the focus on appellate courts, which decisions do not re-evaluate facts, thus there are no trial court **inferential** or **credibility arguments** – very common to the criminal law practice.

Also it has been argued that statutory analysis should be greater, since the system is walking towards a written law tendency – what we have seen before with the partial model penal code ruling adoption (Bergman, 2012, p. 7).

— 2.2 —
Legal issues

Legal analysis is made over the stories, which are the judges' opinions on cases. The parties analyze theses stories, trying to identify the legal mistakes present in lower court's decisions that require a review.

Put it simple: the legal issue is the mistake, the controversy, the supposedly problem in a lower court's decision that is being appreciated by a superior court. "Legal issues are the focus of adversaries' arguments; and decide cases by resolving legal issues" (Bergman, 2012, p. 18).

The legal issue generation, as well as the argumentation construction by the judges, will culminate in a legal principle, a ruling, a solution to all posterior facts regarding that same matter. It is discussed in the opinion's part called "the law of the case".

> **The Law of the Case**: After the opinion has presented the facts, it will then discuss the law. This section of the opinion describes the legal principles that the judge will use to decide the case and reach a particular outcome. In many cases, the law is presented in two stages: first the opinion will discuss the general principles of law that are relevant to the case given its facts, and next the court will apply the law to the facts and reach the court's outcome. (Kerr, 2005, p. 3)

The lawyers' job is, when appealing a lower court's decision, to find and elaborate over the present legal issues, and that is a work that requires study and a bit of creativity. It is necessary to know the law, to formulate the legal issues. For example, the lawyer must know evidence rules so he can identify a case of illegal evidence suppression and turn it into a legal issue to be discussed by higher courts.

Legal issues are originated by abstract principles of law (such as the sufficiency of evidence to establish the accused state of mind in the crime commission), but also by the link of principles to concrete cases. Bergman uses in his book a very elucidating example in this last case. A specific evidence statute provides that previous acts of domestic violence are only admissible in a subsequent domestic violence crime prosecution (that is the legal principle). In a murder case, involving the accused's girlfriend, previous acts of domestic violence were brought to court by the accusation (that is the concrete case) (Bergman, 2012, p. 19).

The legal issue resulting by the link of the concrete case to the legal principle is the possibility of admitting prior acts of domestic violence in the murder case of the accused's partner, more specifically, the legal issue is the following question: "Is murder of a girlfriend an offense involving domestic violence?" (Bergman, 2012, p. 19). That is the problem the court has to solve.

Legal issues are also divided regarding their nature, into doctrinal and application legal issues. In the considered doctrinal ones, appellants sick either a new legal principle creation or the invalidation of existing ones. As to the application legal issues, they relate to existing legal principle's interpretation, based on the concrete case (Bergman, 2012, p. 25). Substantive legal principles relate to rights and obligations, opposed to procedural ones that relate to the process of the decision-making.

The legal issues are not always explicit in a judge's opinion, and usually students recently introduced to the case method have to start analyzing an opinion from its end to the beginning to find it. Usually, in the part where the law is being discussed, the language is "The first issue we have..." (Bergman, 2012, p. 29).

For that, it is interesting comprehending how to read a judicial opinion. Basically, opinions are divided in the following topics: the caption, the case citation, the author of the opinion, the facts of the case, the law of the case, the disposition, concurring and dissenting opinions.

The caption is the name of the case, the citation reveals the year the case was judged and by which court, after that, the author of the opinion brings the justice's last name. In the body of the decision we have the facts of the case, the law of the case – "in this section of the opinion describes the legal principles that the judge will use to decide the case and reach a particular outcome" (Kerr, 2005, p. 3).

Then the opinion brings the disposition, at the end of it, stating what is the court's decision. Decisions, which are not unanimous, may also have a concurrent opinion and/or a dissenting opinion. One of the most important things is to identify all this sections present in a judicial decision.

For that reason, we bring an explained, and already summarized, opinion, identifying all the aspects cited.

Ewing v. California (the caption)

538 U.S. 11 (2003) (the citation)

Opinion of O'CONNOR, J (the author of the opinion)

SUPREME COURT OF THE UNITED STATES
GARY ALBERT EWING, PETITIONER v. CALIFORNIA
ON WRIT OF CERTIORARI TO THE COURT OF APPEAL OF CALIFORNIA, SECOND APPELLATE DISTRICT [March 5, 2003]

JUSTICE O'CONNOR announced the judgment of the Court and delivered an opinion in which THE CHIEF JUSTICE and JUSTICE KENNEDY join.

"In this case, we decide whether the Eighth Amendment prohibits the State of California from sentencing a repeat felon to a prison term of 25 years to life under the State's "Three Strikes and You're Out" law." (legal issue)

The facts of the case

"On parole from a 9-year prison term, petitioner Gary Ewing walked into the pro shop of the El Segundo Golf Course in Los Angeles County on March 12, 2000. He walked out with three golf clubs, priced at $399 a piece, concealed in his pants leg. A shop employee, whose suspicions were aroused when he observed Ewing limp out of the pro shop, telephoned the police. The police apprehended Ewing in the parking lot. Ewing is no stranger to the criminal justice system. In 1984, at the age of 22, he pleaded guilty to theft. The court sentenced him to six months in jail (suspended), three years' probation, and a $300 fine. In 1988, he was convicted of felony grand theft auto and sentenced to one year in jail and three year's probation. After Ewing completed probation, however, the sentencing court reduced the crime to a misdemeanor, permitted Ewing to withdraw his guilty plea, and dismissed the case. In 1990, he was convicted of petty theft with a prior and sentenced to 60 days in the county jail and three years' probation. In 1992, Ewing was convicted of battery and sentenced to 30 days in the county jail and two years' summary probation. One month later, he was convicted of theft and sentenced to 10 days in the county jail and 12 months' probation. In January 1993, Ewing was convicted of burglary and sentenced to 60 days in the county jail and one year's summary probation. In February 1993, he was convicted of possessing drug paraphernalia and sentenced to six months in the county jail and three years' probation. In July 1993, he was convicted of appropriating lost property and sentenced to 10 days in the county jail and two years' summary probation. In September 1993, he was convicted of unlawfully possessing a firearm and trespassing and sentenced to 30 days in the county jail and one year's probation.

In October and November 1993, Ewing committed three burglaries and one robbery at a Long Beach, California, apartment complex over a 5-week period. He awakened one of his victims, asleep on her living room sofa, as he tried to disconnect her videocassette recorder from the television in that room.

When she screamed, Ewing ran out the front door. On another occasion, Ewing accosted a victim in the mailroom of the apartment complex. Ewing claimed to have a gun and ordered the victim to hand over his wallet. When the victim resisted, Ewing produced a knife and forced the victim back to the apartment itself. While Ewing rifled through the bedroom, the victim fled the apartment screaming for help. Ewing absconded with the victim's money and credit cards.

On December 9, 1993, Ewing was arrested on the premises of the apartment complex for trespassing and lying to a police officer. The knife used in the robbery and a glass cocaine pipe were later found in the back seat of the patrol car used to transport Ewing to the police station. A jury convicted Ewing of first-degree robbery and three counts of residential burglary. Sentenced to nine years and eight months in prison, Ewing was paroled in 1999.

Only 10 months later, Ewing stole the golf clubs at issue in this case. He was charged with, and ultimately convicted of, one count of felony grand theft of personal property in excess of $400.

[...]

At the sentencing hearing, Ewing asked the court to reduce the conviction for grand theft, a "wobbler" under California law, to a misdemeanor so as to avoid a three strikes sentence. See ß17(b) (West 1999); ß667(d)(1); ß1170.12(b)(1) (West Supp. 2002). Ewing also asked the trial court to exercise its discretion to dismiss the allegations of some or all of his prior serious or violent felony convictions, again for purposes of avoiding a three strikes sentence.

In the end, the trial judge determined that the grand theft should remain a felony. The court also ruled that the four prior strikes for the three burglaries and the robbery in Long Beach should stand. As a newly convicted felon with two or more "serious" or "violent" felony convictions in his past, Ewing was sentenced under the three strikes law to 25 years to life. The California Court of Appeal affirmed.

Opinion – the law of the case (from Legal Information Institute – Cornell University)

"(a) The Eighth Amendment has a "narrow proportionality principle" that "applies to noncapital sentences." Harmelin v. Michigan, 501 U.S. 957, 996–997 (Kennedy, J., concurring in part and concurring in judgment). The Amendment's application in this context is guided by the principles distilled in Justice Kennedy's concurrence in Harmelin: "[T]he primacy of the legislature, the variety of legitimate penological schemes, the nature of our federal system, and the requirement that proportionality review be guided by objective factors" inform the final principle that the **"Eighth Amendment does not require strict proportionality between crime and sentence [but] forbids only extreme sentences that are 'grossly disproportionate' to the crime."** Id., at 1001. Pp. 8–11.

(b) State legislatures enacting three strikes laws made a deliberate policy choice that individuals who have repeatedly engaged in serious or violent criminal behavior, and whose conduct has not been deterred by more conventional punishment approaches, must be isolated from society to protect the public safety. Though these laws are relatively new, this Court has a longstanding tradition of deferring to state legislatures in making and implementing such important policy decisions. **The Constitution "does not mandate adoption of any one penological theory," id., at 999, and nothing in the Eighth Amendment prohibits California from choosing to incapacitate criminals who have already been convicted of at least one serious or violent crime.** Recidivism has long been recognized as a legitimate basis for increased punishment and is a serious public safety concern in California and the Nation. Any criticism of the law is appropriately directed at the legislature, which is primarily responsible for making the policy choices underlying any criminal sentencing scheme. Pp. 11–15.

(c) In examining Ewing's claim that his sentence is grossly disproportionate, the gravity of the offense must be compared to the harshness of the penalty. Even standing alone, his grand theft should not be taken lightly. The California Supreme Court has noted that crime's seriousness in the context of proportionality review; that it is a "wobbler" is of no moment, for it remains a felony unless the trial court imposes a misdemeanor sentence. The trial judge justifiably exercised her discretion not to extend lenient treatment given Ewing's long criminal history. In weighing the offense's gravity, both his current felony and his long history of felony recidivism must be placed on the scales. Any other approach would not accord proper deference to the policy judgments that find expression in the legislature's choice of sanctions. **Ewing's sentence is justified by the State's public-safety interest in incapacitating and** deterring **recidivist felons, and amply supported by his own long, serious criminal record. He has been convicted of numerous offenses, served nine separate prison terms, and committed most of his crimes while on probation or parole. His prior strikes were serious felonies including robbery and residential burglary. Though long, his current sentence reflects a rational legislative judgment that is entitled to deference.** Pp. 15–18."

Holding

"We hold that Ewing's sentence of 25 years to life in prison, imposed for the offense of felony grand theft under the three strikes law, **is not grossly disproportionate and therefore does not violate the Eighth Amendment's prohibition on cruel and unusual punishments**. The judgment of the California Court of Appeal is affirmed."

Justice O'Connor delivered the opinion of the court, which was joined by Rehnquist, and Kennedy. Justices Scalia and Thomas filed concurring opinions and Justices Stevens, joined by 3 other justices, filed a dissenting opinion.

Ewing had been convicted to previous crimes before, being arrested and convicted of stealing golf clubs (what characterizes recidivism). Since the facts happened in California, the last crime committed by Ewing, under the **wobbler** policy, was considered a felony instead of a misdemeanor, which is a more serious crime, and with that, due to recidivism, he could be judged under the three strike's law. According to this law, the ones who committed two or more "serious" or "violent" felonies can be sentenced to 25 years to life in prison. The stealing of the golf clubs, due to **the value of the stolen products (U$ 1,197,00), was characterized** as a "serious felony".

Ewing's defense appealed, criticizing the prosecution discretion on considering the last crime a felony, instead of a misdemeanor, and stating that the application of a three strikes penalty (25 years to life in prison) violates the eighth amendment prohibition of cruel and unusual punishment, since it is grossly disproportionate to the crime committed by the defendant.

The court rejected the defense's arguments, affirming the lower courts' decision. The judicial opinion follows the simple structure of stories – legal issues – arguments – holding. In the case analyzed, since there were 3 three justices joining the author's opinion and 2 more justices concurring, they had **the majority to affirm the Lower Court decision (5 against 4 dissenting).**

The concurrent opinions agreed to the penalty imposed to Ewing, but for different reasons. Justices Scalia and Thomas have agreed that the petitioner's sentence does not violate the Constitutional principle, but they also think that proportionality is not applied to the prohibition to cruel and unusual punishment. Ewing's sentence would be justified by the public-safety interest regarding recidivist's deterrence and incapacitation.

> Perhaps the plurality should revise its terminology, so that what it reads into the Eighth Amendment is not the unstated proposition that all punishment should be reasonably proportionate to the gravity of the offense, but rather the unstated proposition **that all punishment should reasonably pursue the multiple purposes of the criminal law.** That formulation would make it clearer than ever, of course, that the plurality is not applying law but evaluating policy. Because I agree that petitioner's sentence does not violate the Eighth Amendment's prohibition against cruel and unusual punishments, I concur in the judgment. (Scalia, J. – Concurrent opining in Ewing v. California, 2003; Legal Information Institute, 2021a).

Justice Thomas joined the concurrence stating that he agrees with justice Scalia and in his view, "the Cruel and Unusual Punishments Clause of the Eighth Amendment contains no proportionality principle. See Harmelin v. Michigan, 501 U. S. 957, 967ñ985 (1991)" (Thomas, J. Concurrent opining in Ewing v. California, 2003; Legal Information Institute, 2021a).

On the other hand, the dissenting opinion written by justice Breyer, with whom justices Stevens, Souter and Ginsburg joined dissenting, disagrees with the sentence imposed to the petitioner. In his opinion it is the court's work to determine weather the sentence imposed was proportionate, and that is done by precedent analysis through proportional sentence test. Also, he understands that the Eighth Amendment encompasses proportionality of the penalty to the crime committed in its application. In the present case, he agrees with the petitioner's argument that the sentence was grossly disproportionate.

> This Court's precedent sets forth a framework for analyzing Ewing's Eighth Amendment claim. The Eighth Amendment forbids, as "cruel and unusual punishments", prison terms (including terms of years) that are "grossly disproportionate."
>
> [...]
>
> In Solem v. Helm, 463 U. S. 277 (1983), the Court found grossly disproportionate a somewhat longer sentence imposed on a recidivist offender for triggering criminal conduct that was somewhat less severe. In my view, the differences are not determinative, and the Court should reach the same ultimate conclusion here. [...]
>
> To implement this approach, courts faced with a "gross disproportionality" claim must first make ia threshold comparison of the crime committed and the sentence imposed."
>
> [...]

If a claim crosses that threshold itself, a rare occurrence, then the court should compare the sentence at issue to other sentences "imposed on other criminals" in the same, or in other, jurisdictions. The comparative analysis will "validate" or "invalidate" them.

[...]

A case-by-case approach can nonetheless offer guidance through example. Ewing's sentence is, at a minimum, 2 to 3 times the length of sentences that other jurisdictions would impose in similar circumstances. That sentence itself is **sufficiently long to require a typical offender to spend** virtually all the remainder of his active life in prison. These and the other factors that I have discussed, along with the questions that I have asked along the way, should help to identify "gross disproportionality" in a fairly objective way óat the outer bounds of sentencing. In sum, even if I accept for present purposes the plurality's analytical framework, Ewing's sentence (life imprisonment with a minimum term of 25 years) is grossly disproportionate to the triggering offense conduct of stealing three golf clubs Ewing's recidivism notwithstanding. For these reasons, I dissent (538 U. S. ____ (2003) 3 BREYER, J., dissenting initial judgment that a sentence is grossly disproportionate to a crime.)

This case is already summarized, due to pedagogical purposes, but, in order to be able to really get the important information from cases, it is necessary to learn how to brief them. That is what we are doing in our next topic of study.

Legal Vocabulary Bank

- **Dwelling-house** – "3. Criminal Law. A building, a part of a building, a tent, a mobile home, or another enclosed space that is used or intended for use as a human habitation. [...] now typically includes only the structures connected either directly with the house or by an enclosed passageway" (Garner, 2016 p. 265).
- **Holding** – "A court's determination of a matter of law pivotal to its decision; a principle drawn from such a decision. [...]" (Garner, 2016, p. 357).
- **Respondent** – "The party against whom an appeal is taken; APPELLE* In some appellate courts, the parties are designated as *petitioner* and *respondent*. In most appellate courts in the United States, the parties are designated as appellant or appellee. Often the designation depend on whether the appeal is taken by writ od certiorari (or writ of error) or by direct appeal. [...]" (Garner, 2016, p. 653).
- **Inferential arguments** – circumstantial evidence (as opposed to direct evidence) rests on inferences to be proved. These inferences are objected to argumentation, by both parties, to rule out or reaffirm the evidence at issue. Examples of circumstantial evidence:
    - Witness testimony saying she heard a scream or that she saw the defendant entering the victim's house;

- Fingerprints'
- Blood analysis;
- DNA analysis;
- Ballistics; (Bergman, 2012, p. 46)
- **Wobbler** – "Slang. A crime that can be charged as either a felony or a misdemeanor" (Garner, 2016, p. 384).

— 2.3 —
Briefing cases

Since the volume of reading for law school students are huge, it is essential to learn how to summarize (brief) cases, taking notes of its important parts. On the other hand, rending strait from the source – the judicial decision instead of outlines – is extremely necessary, since the legal reasoning construction and the argumentation strategies are exposed in the opinions. Also, the academic needs to get familiar with legal vocabulary, what is even more important when it comes to international students.

The focus during the case briefing is working with legal reasoning, by deconstructing cases "rhetorically" and reading them critically, by rewriting rationales on the student's own words. (Bergman, 2012, p. 77). The first thing to do when you get the first contact with a new case is a fast reading of it, skimming the text to identify what is being discussed, the parties and who has won.

After that first relaxed reading you can start deepening the knowledge, through a more interested reading. Only after a second or a third reading the student is prepared to star briefing a case. Important to notice that for beginners, especially the ones whose English is the second language and are new to legal vocabulary, the reading is probably going to take more time, and the number of times one is re-reading the case will be higher.

A case brief brings the following information: case name, facts, procedural history, legal issues, holding, reasoning, and disposition.

Facts are important, not only to comprehend the case discussed and imagine legal issues, but also because they work as the basis for future application of the holding, to cases which facts are the same as the one discussed. It is important to take notes of determinative facts, that meaning, the ones the court used to justify its decision (Bergman, 2012, p. 78). If those facts were different the result of the judgment would also be.

The procedural history will summarize the formal litigation. The legal issue section would identify the problems discussed by the opinion – usually each legal issue is related to one legal principle. The holding is the court answer to an issue. The reasoning brings the explanation made through arguments to the holdings. The disposition gives the final position of the court, if it has reversed or affirmed the lower court's decision.

The case studied in the previous topic, originally, has many more pages than the ones we have brought, especially if we consider the concurring and dissenting opinions. But even with the case as it is presented it is possible and necessary to brief it. The result would be something like this:

- **Case name**: Ewing v. California (2003)
- **Facts**: Ewing was convicted of grand theft after stealing golf clubs, once the crime was a wobbler under de CA law, what allowed the application of the three strikes law – with undetermined sentence from 25 years to life – due to Ewing's recidivism (he had already been convicted of robbery and three burglaries).
- **Procedural history**: Court judge denied reducing the wobbler felony to a misdemeanor to avoid three strikes law. The Court of Appeal affirmed the trial judge sentence. The Supreme Court of California has denied reviewing the case. The case was filed at the US Supreme Court – writ of certiorari.
- **Legal issue**: Can the Eighth Amendment prohibit State of California to sentencing a repeat felon to a prison term of 25 years to life under the three strikes law?
- **Holding**: The Ewing's sentence of 25 years to life in prison, imposed for the offense of felony grand theft under the three strikes law, is not grossly disproportionate and therefore does not violate the Eighth Amendment's prohibition on cruel and unusual punishments.

- **Reasoning**:
  * **Principles for 8th a. application**: "[T]he primacy of the legislature, the variety of legitimate penological schemes, the nature of our federal system, and the requirement that proportionality review be guided by objective factors".
  * Eighth Amendment does not require strict proportionality between crime and sentence [but] forbids only extreme sentences that are grossly disproportionate' to the crime.
  * Ewing's sentence is justified by the State's public-safety interest in incapacitating and deterring recidivist felons, and amply supported by his own long, serious criminal record. Not grossly disproportionate.
- **Disposition**: The judgment of the California Court of Appeal is affirmed.

The same briefing example may be used to the concurrent or dissenting opinions. The words in a case brief may be abbreviated, and also can be used only the indispensible ones, so it gets shorter and faster to be made. Here, we opted to use the complete sentences and words, to make sure the reader gets the idea.

Also, it is possible to organize a comments section, in which the student can organize thoughts of his own regarding the decision – agreeing or not to it, formulating questions to be asked in class, taking notes of insights, among others.

Finally, it is very common for beginners to read and brief the cases and get to class thinking they are prepared. Once the class discussion begins and the professor start making questions about the case, the students realize they lack information, they did not get the main idea, or that they simply did not understand the case.

Perfection comes with practice, and working attention and continuously on the cases' analysis is the only way to get good at briefing them. But, to help insecure students, making them able to go to classes calmer, there are some websites that may help. There are some law webpages designed to give organized case briefs. That may be useful for the student to check if he is in the right path, at least at the very beginning. But that would only be of certain help if it were used as a checking source, after the academic has done the hard work of reading and trying to brief the cases himself. Otherwise, it would not help developing argumentative nor legal analysis skills. Legal argumentation is our next topic of study.

> Brady v. Maryland. Available at: <https://supreme.justia.com/cases/federal/us/373/83/>. Acess on April, 7th, 2021.
>
> Brady v. Maryland. **Case Brief**. Avaliable at: <https://www.lexisnexis.com/community/casebrief/p/casebrief-brady-v-maryland>. Acess on April, 7th, 2021.
>
> Brady v. Maryland. **Oyez**. Avaliable at: <https://www.oyez.org/cases/1962/490>. Acess on April, 7th, 2021.

— 2.4 —

Argument strategies

From what we have seen so far it is easy to comprise that the legal activity is based on argumentation, both written and oral, despite the fact that the first type is more commonly practiced.

The dialectic method is very much present when developing arguments and counterarguments in the legal practice. Historically it was instituted as a method with Plato, and can be summarized in three concepts, **thesis, antithesis** and **synthesis**, that would work in the following way:

Image 2.1 – Dialectic method

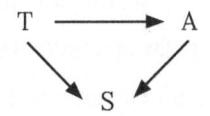

```
    T ────▶ A
     ╲    ╱
      ╲  ╱
       S
```

Transposing this line of reasoning to the legal practice, we have arguments (thesis), counterarguments (antithesis) and judicial opinion (synthesis). When formulating and developing an argument, it is of the most importance, as in necessary, to bring to the analysis the important counterarguments (antithesis) existing to your thesis. This counterarguments must be addressed and whenever possible, defeated by stronger arguments.

This rational is not only true in the legal practice, in trial or with the appealing procedures. The academic life is also marked with this characteristic, the need of addressing research, discussions and academic work dialectically.

We have previously established that the case method requires two main tasks, those being: to identify the controversial(s) legal issue(s) and to develop arguments. In the last topic we talked about the first task, regarding legal issues. Now, we will concentrate on crafting arguments. We will focus on common types of arguments in this topic, also brought by Bergman in his book "Cracking the case method" (Bergman, 2012, p. 33).

Arguments can be formulated based on many sources, since common experience, going through precedential and public policy arguments, until slippery slope types – not recommended, as we are going to see.

Common experience arguments are based in one's life experience, since all of us grew up is social groups, what implicates argumentation to get to a consensus, and that happens from childhood on, specially for those who have brothers at home. The daily argumentation practices go on, changing environments as we get older, from home to school, from school to college, from college to the working environment, and so on. This persuasive daily argumentation is also used in the legal practice.

But there are a variety of sources that can originate arguments, not only the law and judicial opinions, but also law review articles, legal encyclopedias, practitioner journals, among others, serving as secondary sources for argumentation development.

Precedential arguments have already been discussed by us. As we have seen, precedents can be resumed to prior decision emanated by a court in the same hierarchy, or above, the court deciding the case. To find a precedent compatible to solve an intended legal issue means having a really strong argument against your opponent.

In this point it is necessary to open a parenthesis to discuss the policy of *stare decisis*, which stipulates the precedent practice and its biding force to future decisions. It aims law stability, continuity and predictability of the justice system. However, *stare decisis* is not absolute and it can be abandoned "if judges conclude that a claimed precedent was wrongly decided" (Bergman, 2012, p. 38). That was expressed in the Ewing *v.* California case, analyzed before.

Justice Scalia, in the concurring opinion, wrote he could accept the contrary holding of a case that is a precedent of the court, if he understood that was the correct decision – which, in his opinion, was not.

Out of respect for the principle of stare decisis, I might nonetheless accept the contrary holding of Solem v. Helm, 463 U. S. 277 (1983) that the Eighth Amendment contains a narrow proportionality principle, if I felt I could intelligently apply it. This case demonstrates why I cannot. [...]" -538 U.S. ____ (2003) 1 SCALIA, J., concurring in judgment (Cornell Law School, 2003)

Relating to the possibility the court can abandon the *stare decisis* policy, another strategy of the other party – that does not benefit the precedent, is the precedent-avoiding argument, in order to convince the court the precedent case does not control the one at issue. Reasons to abandon precedent are usually related to "changes in cultural mores, social conditions, technology and even legal policies [...]" (Bergman, 2012, p. 37).

Another argument type is the consequentialist one, in which the consequences that may follow the legal outcome desired are used persuasively. The author uses the Miranda decision to exemplify this type of argumentation. The Miranda Rule stipulates that police officers have to tell suspects about their right to remain silent and to have counsel orientation (Miranda v. Arizona, 1966).

The majority opinion in the case used many consequentialist arguments in favor of giving the warning, such as safeguard the trial process and reduce police abuse. On the opposite side, the dissenting opinion used consequentialists' arguments against the obligation of giving the warning. The reduction of confessions, the harm to crime control efforts and the frustration of criminals "who are anxious to be convicted", are among the arguments used (Miranda v. Arizona, 1966).

Analogical arguments encompass precedent arguments, since they are based on pointing similarities and distinctions between circumstances. Social policy arguments are usually present when a statute application is being discussed. They raise questions such as the policy behind the law or what the rule wants to protect or preserve. Modern policy arguments would be present in drugs use legalization, euthanasia, abortion, and many other conducts that are considered by part of society as an individual right.

The author characterizes inferential arguments, analyzed before, historical arguments, linguistic arguments, and two other very interesting types, Slippery Slope and Sure-Fire Losing Rhetorical Strategies (Miranda v. Arizona, 1966). Slippery Slope arguments are represented by a first small idea or innovation that might lead to a significant (negative) effect. Behind the rational there is the idea that the acceptance of the argument presented would open the gate for future expansions of the rationale, which are not welcomed.

As an argumentative strategy, sometimes it is considered prudent not to go for all the thesis existing and wanted to be recognized by the judges, but to centralize the argumentation in specific points that are more sure to be considered by the court, in order to avoid the slippery slope effect.

Hypothetically, lets imagine, centuries ago, when native people of a determined colonialized region were not considered citizens, since that was a very prejudiced society. A portion this countries' citizens was not in agreement to this policy, and decided to fight to establish these native people some rights, considering them citizens.

Due to the conservative nature of the court, the strategy used was electing arguments to the concession of some specific rights, rather than making a vibrant speech about how the Native people should be considered citizens – what would be denied by the court and no advance would be made in granting the people more rights. Among the arguments related to the right to schooling, for example, was how it would benefit employees to have more educated labor force available.

Finally, Sure-Fire Losing Rhetorical Strategies are made up with arguments that do not provide rational reasons; which could be very common in jury trials, with attorneys appealing to the "good sense" of the jurors, and to their "good hearts" when making a decision, without appreciating or exploring the existing evidence on the case. This argumentation type should be avoided under all circumstances.

Synthesis

In this chapter we have covered the case study method, understanding the importance of the judicial opinion reading the development of legal analysis and argumentation skills, also being important to learn legal vocabulary – in case of international students that importance is heightened.

We have studied the judicial opinion structure and in what topics it is divided, pointing to the importance of finding the legal issue discussed and the ruling resulting from it. After that we dedicated ourselves to learning the briefing case methodology, as that is an important tool in extracting the essential information of a judicial opinion.

Finally, we have moved on to the discussion of argumentative strategies and how they can help both, academically and professionally, those who relate to the legal field.

Chapter 3

Legal writing

Writing can be a tough exercise. Putting down our thoughts in words in a clear and coherently way requires attention, grammar knowledge and a vast vocabulary, so the reading of it does not get repetitive and tiring.

When it comes to legal writing the obstacles get greater, since we have to deal with legalisms, formal language, statutory language, also being very careful to the meaning of the message we want to send – what is put in paper must reflect exactly the writer's intention, needing the writer to worry in leaving no margin for double interpretation.

For that reason, modern legal writing demands clarity, objectivity and accuracy, without losing the formality inherent to the profession or to the academic research and practice.

We have previously discussed some communicative skills, the language preference when dealing with legal English, also comprehending different argument types. In the present topic we will add to that knowledge writing principles of the English language, aiming to demonstrate what constitutes a good writing, in the academic and the legal professional contexts.

The discussion will dedicate to address questions of persuasive writing, legal drafting, document design and important points regarding writing methods, inspired by the thoughts of Bryan A. Garner, in his book *Legal Writing in Plain English* (2013).

— 3.1 —
Writing well

No matter what type of legal writing you are handling with- they may vary from memos and briefs, to contracts and statutes, with a range of legal documents in between, there are three essential good writing principles that the writer must follow: you must frame your thoughts, phrase your sentences and choose correctly the words you are using. In this topic we are analyzing each of these principles and their developments.

Deciding exactly what points to explore when writing can be daring. But what comes next, after deciding what topics to address, is equally hard, that being expressing them coherently, using arguments to support your ideas and exerting the adequate reasoning.

Writing an academic paper or a legal piece is completely different than writing a novel, where there are almost no limits bedside's the author's imagination. In the first case, structure and language rules must be followed, but besides that, your ideas must be anchored in the existing scientific theories, statutes, and precedent, among others, which have to be cited. The writer's opinion is usually of none importance, unless on a conclusion basis.

But going back to the need of framing your ideas, being objective, cutting of the excessive words in a sentence, is a first step for an effective legal writing. In order to organize tour thoughts, a nonlinear outlining is suggested by Garner, that would work as a brainstorming, but in a more organized way. (Garner, 2013, p. 32). The reason for doing that is the writing process begins even before you start exercising the verb, when there are still no sentences or paragraphs.

So the process starts with the ideas, moving to ordering these thoughts – preparing an outlining, than drafting the written version based on that outline. Finally, it will be the time to work on the final version of the written paper (Garner, 2013, p. 32). The author's example of a nonlinear outline is very interesting.

After choosing the project's name that is centered in the document, the ideas, as many as you can think of, go in the branches. The secondary or supportive ideas go branching of the main one.

Called *whirlybird*, the most popular nonlinear outline looks like the following.

Image 3.1 – Whirlybird outline

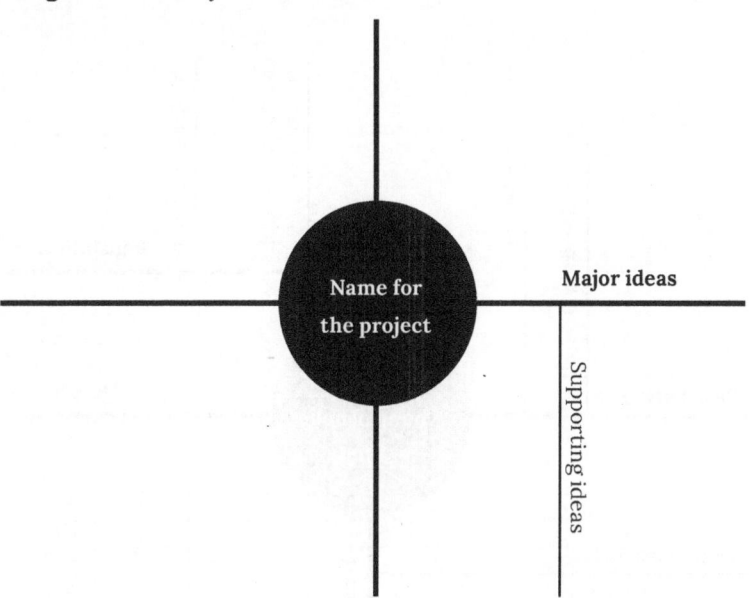

Source: Based on Garner, 2013.

Lets create a real scenario to put that idea in practice. Imagine someone is writing about trying young people as adults, a writing theme that will follow us through the next topic's examples. One possible nonlinear outline could be:

Image 3.2 – Whirlybird outline in practice

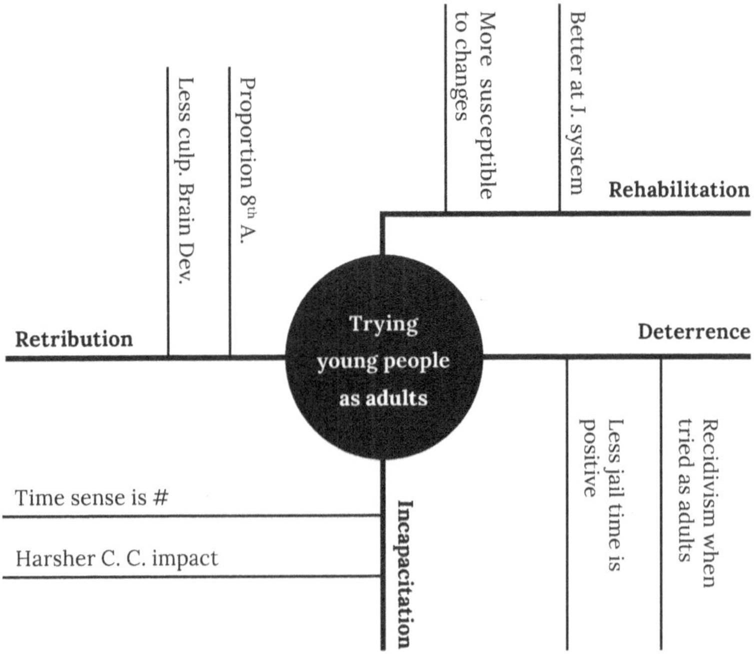

```
                                    Better at J. system
                            More susceptible to changes
                    Proportion 8th A.
            Less culp. Brain Dev.
                                                    Rehabilitation
Retribution                  ( Trying                  Deterrence
                              young people
                              as adults )
                                                    Recidivism when
                                                    tried as adults
                                    Less jail time is positive
Time sense is #
Harsher C. C. impact
                            Incapacitation
```

Source: Based on Garner, 2013.

Just to illustrate some of the arguments existing against trying young people as adults, we brought the main ideas that official penologycal goals (such as deterrence, rehabilitation, incapacitation and retribution) are not achieved by doing so. As secondary ideas, to support our arguments, we indicated studies and statistics that corroborate with our arguments, also proving that the practice has terrible effects on the youth (recidivism, proportion, treatment options, among others).

Of course there are many other arguments and supportive ideas to indicate on the matter. Also, we have not addressed in our outline above possible counterarguments, that being, the arguments existing in favor of trying young people as adults, what is absolutely necessary in a legal discussion, or in an academic work. That will be done next.

The intention here is showing the benefits of that outline, which helps in the creativity process, through the unpretentious idea's formulation. It helps the writer to get started, mapping the thoughts, elucidating the text's key points, also making easily to decide what ideas to really pursue (Garner, 2013, p. 32).

After organizing the ideas like we have shown, the following steps are drafting the written version of the text, for later, making the final version of it, which are much simpler tasks. Also, the chances of having a text that follows a logical sequence (chronologically and sequentially) are greater if the outline is made.

When the writing time takes place, in order to organize the text points, making it clearer to the reader, one suggestion is dividing the writing into sections and subsections, using headings (Garner, 2013, p. 40). A good example of sections and subsection, linking with the outline example given, would be:

In practice

Trying young people as adults.

1. **The arguments against the rational**
    a. Fighting Recidivism
        a.1. Rates are higher when juveniles are tried as adults;
        a.2. Less time in jail is positive when it comes to juveniles.
    b. Jail time for rehabilitation
        b.1. Juveniles are more susceptible to changes – faster;
        b.2. Programs are better at the Juvenile system.
    c. Retribution
        c.1. Proportion – 8th a. violation;
        c.2. Diminished culpability due to incomplete brain development.
    d. Incapacitation
        d.1. Time sense is different for kids and teenagers;
        d.2. Harsher impact of collateral consequences.

2. **Arguments in favor of the rational**
    a. No harsher sentences are given in adult courts;
    b. The youth commits heinous crimes;
    c. Teenagers are co-opted by adults to commit crimes;
    d. Kids are more sophisticated now a days;
    e. Light sentences do not teach.

When writing the text it is also important to phrase the sentences. That means you should only use the needed words – Garner indicates a 20-word sentence as good one. Also, it is indicated to pay attention to the parallelism use (Garner, 2013, p. 40).

In practice

- Use parallelism correctly
  - ✓ Prefer: The students discussed the case jointly and politely. **OR** The students discussed the case in a joint and polite manner.
  - ✗ Avoid: The students discussed the case jointly and in a polite manner.
- correlative conjunctions:
  - ✓ Both... and
  - ✓ Either... or
  - ✓ Neither... nor
  - ✓ Not only... but also

It is important giving preference to active voice, instead of the passive one, also preferring positive to negative statements.
  - ✓ Prefer: The individual should be 18 to be legally able to drink;
  - ✗ Avoid: Drinking cannot be done by anyone under 18.

Another very important aspect of good writing is the word choosing, specially in legal writing, since the formal environment, with the use of legalisms, may lead to an unnecessary and tiring jargon use. The author brings good examples of avoidable jargons in his book such as *case sub judice*, that could be changed to *this case*; *inasmuch as*, could become *because*; *prior to* means *before*, among others (Garner, 2013, p. 60).

Also, the author recommends using strong verbs, since the verbs *be* often lacks force. Change the verb "be" to different ones, stronger ones, whenever possible (Garner, 2013, p. 60). The main idea is the writing must be fluid, speakable, relaxed and natural – the use of connectors at the beginning of the sentences may help with that.

If you get used to framing your thoughts, phrasing your sentences and choosing correctly the words you are using, your chances of writing a legal document and constructing a strong legal argument are highly increased. But this is not enough to achieve success. In the next topic we will cover some principles regarding persuasive writing.

— 3.2 —
Writing persuasively

In the legal environment, writing well is essential but what you write must be not only grammatically correct but also persuasively impacting. You, as a lawyer, have to convince (the judge, the justices, or the other party, for example) that what you stand for is correct.

Garner lists five goals of persuasive writing, which are: a) "Get your point across quickly with a concrete summary up front, b) Focus the analysis or argument, c) Make it interesting, d) Supply smooth transitions and e) Quote smartly and deftly" (Garner, 2103, p. 134).

In order to achieve them, it is recommended to write a three-part text, with short and connected paragraphs, leading in quotations, moving citations to footnotes and, finally, dealing with possible counterarguments (Garner, 2013, p. 134).

Every text should be divided in three parts: 1) an introduction, 2) the middle and 3) the closing part. It is in the introduction part where the writer brings the precise points and arguments discussed in the text. This is the section where you make the question you want to answer by the end of your reasoning.

The middle part is the core of the text, consisting in the reasoning to the ideas that prove your conclusion. This is the part where you deal with any possible counterarguments, using the dialectical method, as discussed before. Here, the use of headings and subheadings are very important, such as showed in the previous topic.

The closing part of a text is the place to sum up the arguments. In here it is advisable to bring back the main points discussed, defining what the conclusion or decision should be and the reasons for that. It is recommended to answer the question from the introduction.

Contextualizing the issue discussed is also important, summarizing it before getting into the details, introducing the paragraphs with a topic sentence is a good way of doing it. Also regarding the paragraphs, they must be connected throughout the text, and that task might be easier with the use of pointing words (*this, that, these, those*) and connectives (*in addition, for example, however, in the same way, in other words, as a result, as a matter of fact, that is, to sum up, finally*).

These paragraphs should be short, having three to eight sentences, and any quotations that might be inserted in the text should be leaded-in, in an assertively way.

In practice

- ✘ Avoid: "The accused stated that: [quotation]"
- ✓ Prefer: "Contrary to what the accusation stated, the accused brought to discussion two different issues regarding the statute in force: [quotation]".

It is also interesting moving citations into footnotes. Finally, but most importantly, your text must address possible counterarguments, as already mentioned. You must show the reader you acknowledge the best objections to your point of view, and, using the dialectical method, you must really try to rebut them.

Following with the issue discussed in this chapter, trying young people as adults, we are making available an example of a three-part text containing the observations made, so the reader can appreciate how those rules and principles of good writing are applicable.

In practice

Trying juveniles as adults.

The present discussion regards weather trying a juvenile in an adult court should be an option to the state in cases of violent or serious crimes. Whatever the penologycal goals of punishment chosen by a given system are, empirical studies support the contra productiveness of sentencing a juvenile as an adult weather seeking their deterrence, rehabilitation, retribution or incapacitation (1). That practice results in clear violation of the 8th Amendment (2) and the prohibition of cruel and unusual punishment, also taking away the burden of the state of making possible children development (3) in society.

(1) If the punishment goals aim deterrence and rehabilitation, studies prove that sentencing the youth for longer imprisonment periods or with higher fines, entailing to more severe collateral

Write a three part text – intro - brings the precise points (arguments) being discussed and the question to be answered.

effects, are not the best option. That is because, when it comes to rehabilitation, teenagers are more susceptible to changes than adults and the access to treatment and rehabilitee options are better in the juvenile system – not o say they are usually not existent in the adult system. However, in the case of deterrence, it is proved not work very well among the youth once they are more inclined to the commitment of inconsequent actions – inclusive because of brain underdevelopment and immaturity related to the young age. Also, teenagers have higher recidivism rates when tried as adults then when tried in juvenile courts.

> Middle: argumentation. Discuss the possible counterarguments, answering them – dialectical method

Opposed to this arguments, are the facts that no harsher or longer sentences are being given to minors when they are tried in adult courts. Also, the end result of a heinous crime remains the same, no matter what the age of the perpetrator is and the justice system depends upon holding perpetrators responsible for their actions. Also, there are supporters of the idea that kids today are more sophisticated at a younger age; they understand the implications of violence and how to use violent weapons.

All these arguments deserve careful attention. It is not only a matter of how harsh the sentences imposed to a teenager tried as an adult are – despite studies proving that juveniles convicted of murder are more likely to receive a life sentence than adults – but also the environment these kids are subjected to while imprisoned. The lack of access to treatment and rehabilitee options is only one of the disadvantages of the adult system.

The interaction with adult criminals – which may lead the teen's career development in the criminal system - is usually intertwined with violence and all kinds of abuses. Guards are not trained to deal with young offenders and the system was not build with the idea of rehabilitation and reinsertion in mind. In connection to that, scientific studies prove that the human complete mental development, including the full capacitation of making free decisions, only occurs at the age of 21 – no matter how sophisticated the kids nowadays are.

Studies also show that juvenile violation is strictly linked to family structure and both, school and work environments. Actually, the most closely related factor to child violation is the presence of friends or family members in gangs. The whole process shows the need for capable measures to be taken in order for breaking the violence trivialization and its cycle. Actions in the field of education, as an example, have been shown to be positive in diminishing the adolescent's vulnerability towards crime and violence. Because reducing the age for criminal responsibility – or trying children as adults – is treating the effect and not the causes of crimes and criminality.

(1) Now, if the punishment goals aim retribution and incapacitation – instead of deterrence and rehabilitation – trying kids and adolescents in adult courts violates the principle of proportionality and may also result in the (2) violation of the 8th amendment and the prohibition of unusual and cruel punishment.

Despite the results reached in the cases analyzed, the justices decisions mentioned that "[...] punishment for crime should be graduated and proportioned to the offender and the offense", and that the proportionality of punishment is viewed "[...] according to the evolving standards of decency that mark the progress of a maturing society".

It was also mentioned that children are different from adults and "[...] because juveniles have diminished culpability and greater prospects for reform, they are less deserving of the most severe punishments". Finally it was stated that juvenile offenders whose crime reflects irreparable corruptions are rare (Legal Information Institute, 2021b).

For an adult - who should be capable to suppress at list most part of the human aggressive instinct and who should be able to performing according to society's rules, a life without parole sentence can be considered an unusual and cruel punishment. For a teenager, who - biologically speaking - should have at least 50 more years of life ahead, LWOP seems extreme harsher. Even when LWOP is not the case, the sense of time for a teenager is completely different. Years go by much slower in their perception. They may really see three years in prison as lifetime.

Furthermore, the impact of the collateral consequences on the youth are harsher and must be sustained by them for a much longer period than an adult - who will live shorter, probably. Such as in life without parole sentencing, the case of retribution is not as strong with a minor as with an adult when the right to parole is conceded – and even among adults, the retribution is not showing itself a practical idea, since the cases of recidivism are only getting more current.

The counterarguments used against these rationales involve the mistaken idea that light sentences don't teach kids the lesson they need to learn: If someone commits a terrible crime, he will spend a considerable part of his life in jail. Also it is argued that harsh sentencing acts as a deterrent to kids who are considering committing crimes. Trying children as adults has coincided with lower rates of juvenile crimes.

_{Citation: moved to footnotes.}

The fact that kids tried in juvenile courts have lower chances of recidivism deconstructs the arguments above, in addiction to the facts that deterrence doesn't work well in the young under 21, as they have limited control over their own environment, that the lengthiest possible incarceration will make juveniles serve more years and a greater percentage of their lives in prison than an adult offender and that juveniles convicted of murder are more likely to receive a life sentence than adults – showing their susceptibility for abuses by the system.

Despite the penologycal theories adopted to try kids and teenagers in adult courts, some rationales against this practice are common to all of them. In the first place it is argued that the law cannot be based on the exception. Youth violence is an exception; kids or teenagers commit only around 16% of violent crimes.

(3) Secondly, juveniles are supposed to be protected by the state and trying kids as adults is a way of immunizing the state from its responsibility (in the front end with home, food, education, leisure and at the back end with ways to rehabilitate kids and reinsert them at the less costly way possible). Furthermore, juveniles are, most of the time, victims and not offenders. On average, juveniles (ages 12-17) were more than twice as likely as adults (age 18 or older) to be the victim of violent crimes. Among juveniles aged 17 or younger, blacks were five times as likely as whites to be the victim of a homicide.

Finally, (2) sentencing and incarcerating juveniles as adults may be considered an eighth amendment violation, due to many of the reasons stated above, from mental partial development of teenagers to the abuses they are subjected in jail.

Closer: sum up the argument. Bring back main points. Point what the decision should be and the reasons for that. Answer the question from the introduction.

There is no other conclusion than the fact that juveniles should never be submitted to adult court judgment, despite the gravity of the offense committed, since that practice would not positively impact on better crime deterrence results nor the ones regarding the defendant's rehabilitation. On the contrary, adult court judgments would have a negative impact on the penological goals, submitting the young defendant to cruel and unusual punishment, in violation to the Eight Amendment.

In this text the three part division is really clear, an introduction with the question the writer intends to answer and the arguments he is going to use, a middle part with the arguments development, also being present the counterarguments to the rational pointed. Finally, there is a conclusion answering the question from the beginning and pointing the main reasoning.

Citations and secondary information were moved to footnotes, paragraphs were short and connected through the use of connectives (*furthermore, however, in addition, despite of*, among others).

— 3.3 —
Legal drafting

It is part of the legal activity drafting documents. A draft is a preliminary version of a text or document, that could be, and probably will be, subjected to changes and adaptations. In this session we will give attention to document drafting, such as contracts and agreements – not being these type of documents restricted to those.

A document draft is related to future events, an intended negotiation or acquisition, for example. There are usually, at least, two parties interested in the document's contents, and they almost ever have opposing interests (buyer and seller, *landlord and tenant*, supplier and purchaser, employer and employee, just to mention a few). For this reason, a document draft, such as a contract draft, is read adversarilly, and should present no mistakes, despite its preliminary character.

Based on Garner's principles, we have summarized some of the main ideas regarding a good legal drafting (Garner, 2013, p. 230). A draft should be objective and clear, the words should be technically chosen, and it must an organized document, neither difficult nor tiring to read. In order to easily get that there are some advice that could be useful.

First recommended thing is to avoid high legalism style, giving preference to the plain English, as we have discussed before. Jargons should be avoided, as much as excessive words, besides over formal language should be prevented.

Secondly, the draft maker should keep in mind who his audience is, in order to direct his writing to those people, using a familiar an comprehensible language to them. The documents might be designated to general clients, with no technical skills, or lawyers, investors, legal committees, a group of people who have specific know how in different fields.

Another advice regards the document structure and organization. It is interesting organizing the discussed points in order of importance, in a descending scale. Here, as well as in any legal writing, giant paragraphs should be broken down, using a lot of numerated information. Again, the use heading and subtitles are important. Garner (2013) suggests choosing numbers over letters when numerating information.

As to the legal text, the writer must not use the word *shall*, preferring *will*, for reasons of ambiguity that may be created by that word used. The *and/or* also must be excluded from the text, since it can be interpreted both inclusively and exclusively, depending on the good faith of the opposite part. Regarding to that issue, there is transcript below of a case where the use of *and/or* was very criticized.

> Florida Supreme Court: "Criticizing use of "and/or" in a civil petition because imprecise, but not holding it to be reversible error":
>
> [...] distinguished company of lawyers who have condemned its use. **It is one of those inexcusable barbarisms which** were sired by indolence and damned by indifference, and **has no more place in legal terminology** than the vernacular of Uncle Remus has in Holy Writ. **I am unable to divine how such senseless jargon becomes current.** The coiner of it certainly had **no appreciation for terse and concise law English**
>
> (Cochrane v. Fla. E. Coast Rwy. Co., 1932)

Remember, a document drafting must be objective, clear, giving no margins to double meaning. It has to be organized, and the readers must be able to go easily throw the document, finding the topics they want to discuss, even though they don't follow the reading order – drafts are usually not read thoroughly, from top to bottom.

— 3.4 —
Document designing

The objective of producing a readable document is precisely maximizing the retrieval of information on the reader's part. And the page layout has an impact on that. Let's analyze the tips elaborated by Garner on this matter (Garner, 2013, p. 249).

The writer should choose a readable typeface – in Brazil the most popular academic and professional typefaces are Arial or Times New Roman, size 12. As a methodological tip, rather than worrying about which of these you should choose, it is important to use the same typeface through the document, even in the footnotes citations. A change of typeface is easily recognized and might indicate the writer lacked reviewing the draft or did it without paying the appropriate attention.

Making the draft readable also means, besides the language used, employing the organization tips discussed before – such as bullets, headings, small paragraphs, footnote citation, as well as applying spaces to break up dense pages. An organized document may stimulate the reader to actually read it, paying attention to the information.

Call attention to what you consider important ideas in the text by highlighting them. Bullet points, new headings or subheadings may be useful. Avoid using all capital letters. When the document elaborated is long, containing more than six pages, make a table of contents, so the reader can easily go throughout the document.

Elaborating a pleasant document to be read – that meaning, well written and organized, clear on its information, easy to go through and good to look at – will improve the chances that the information provided will be attentively appreciated and retrieved, and its persuasive capacity will be improved. That is the goal of any law professional.

The legal texts present some recurrent vocabulary, such as prepositional phrases, verb-noun collocations and particular verbs. There are some examples listed next.

- **Legal common vocabulary:**
    - ✓ Revoke – withdraw
    - ✓ Tem – name
    - ✓ To entail – to involve
    - ✓ To typify – to be an example of
    - ✓ To recover – to regain
    - ✓ Prefer – opt for
    - ✓ Enforceable – valid
    - ✓ Penalties – additional fees
    - ✓ Obtain – get
    - ✓ Notify – inform

- **Verb-noun collocation**
    - ✓ Violate – a law
    - ✓ Call – a meeting
    - ✓ Overturn – a decision
    - ✓ Gain – representation
    - ✓ Conduct – affairs

- **Prepositional phrases**

    ✓ In terms of: with respect or relation to; as indicated by.
    ✓ In the course of: while, during.
    ✓ By way of: for the purpose of; by the route through.
    ✓ In response to: as an answer to; in reply to.

    Source: Krois-Linder, 2009.

— 3.5 —
Writing methods

Well, we have come to a point where all the basic principles of a good writing are on the table. If you put them in practice you will certainly have a good piece of work in hands. However, one really important step will be missing, even if you follow all the advices given previously. That would be the final analysis of your document, the last thing to do to make sure you have a readable work. That meaning, if you followed all the steps – brainstorming, outlining, drafting and making the final written version of your text, it is time for you to edit your script.

You can do this by re-reading your text, correcting easy and simple mistakes, changing repeated or unfitted words, moving paragraphs for better cohesion, inserting connectives for paragraph linking and text flow, just to mention a few examples. That is true even for non-legal texts. There are professional writers, such as Valter Hugo Mãe, who is a Portuguese novelist, and affirmed to read his texts out loud, in order to check for repeated words, mistakes and text flow – what constantly makes him hoarse during the writing process. That might be a good tactic for legal texts, since the writing must be natural and speakable, as we have seen.

It is the time to analyze deeper issues, like if you have made your point clear from the beginning of the text, if you have addressed all the strong counterarguments existing, if you ended the text answering the question from the beginning, for example. Asking someone else to read you work may be a good idea, since after working for a long period on a text your reading may get flawed. The main questions to be asked about you text are: have you been clear, objective, brief, fluid, accurate, original, practical?

A grammatically correct writing must follow all this. Do not be lazy to search for unfamiliar words on the dictionary or to search for synonyms, avoiding being repetitive. Also, have a good grammar book available, so you can have a back up when it comes, for example, to punctuation rules. And remember, writing is a skill that requires practice, but also requires reading. To be a good writer one must be a good reader.

Synthesis

In this chapter we have discussed principles of good writing, based on the work of Bryan A. Garner, *Legal Writing in Plain English*. Garner is also the editor in chief of the legal dictionary *Black Law's Dictionary*, very much used here as a source for legal vocabulary, concepts and principles.

According to the author, as developed on the previous pages, legal writing involves more than knowing the legal English, what is absolutely necessary but not sufficient. A good written text or document requires the observation of some important writing principles, which were discussed in the chapter. The writing process must be taken as a whole, and it stars before putting the words into a paper. The idea generation, the outlining, the drafting, the text final version and its revision are all very important parts in the writing process.

Between them, there are persuasive writing principles that must take place, such as objectivity, accuracy and organization of the text, which has to be divided in an introduction, middle and a conclusion, with its developments. Contextualization of issues discussed is also necessary. Legalism and unnecessary jargons must be avoided, and all that in order to have a pleasant readable legal text.

Chapter 4

Introduction to the American Criminal System

It is very common among international academic students interested in learning Legal English the will of also comprehending the international legal system and learning legal and court vocabulary. I believe we have covered most of that in the previous chapters.

However, students also desire to learn statutory language, and, in the case of those who are interested in the criminal law, to have a notion about criminal law and procedure rules. As mentioned before, it is also easier to understand the language and retain vocabulary when dealing with objective examples.

For all of these reasons, in this chapter we will discuss the criminal law and procedure in the US, in an introductory way, also reflecting about some other aspects of the criminal justice system in that country, as the prison privatization policies.

— 4.1 —
Introduction to criminal law

Talking about an American criminal law is a difficult task, once there are innumerous statutes and penal codes that are valid in the US territory, since the legislative power on the matter belongs to the states. Rules, crime classification, criminal sanctions, criminal liability ages are some of the aspects of the penal law that may vary from state to state.

The intention here is to analyze some peculiarities and other generalities of the criminal justice system. We are using both state and federal rules as reference, indicating which one is being discussed every time.

As we have seen, the Model Penal Code has had a great influence in state codes, specially regarding their general part, which will be analyzed by us in some aspects. As to crime classifications, we will discuss generally admitted concepts, in most states, indicating the specific state statute when discussing a particular case.

In addition to that, we are going to address the concept of misdemeanors and what part they play in the criminal system. After that we will throw light over the pre-trial and trial proceedings, as well as talking about prison privatization policies.

— 4.1.1 —
Penal statutes: general part

In this section we are taking the California Penal Code as a reference to understand crime definition, excuses and justifications, culpability and some of the valid criminal law principles. From now on, when cited, the California Penal Code will be referred as CPC.

The CPC is divided in four parts: 1) Of crimes and punishments; 2) Of criminal procedures; 3) Of state prison and county jails; 4) Of prevention of crimes and apprehension of criminals. When it comes to the "Crimes and Punishments" part, the following titles are encompassed:

- Of offenses against the sovereignty of the state;
- Of crimes by and against the executive power of the state;
- Of crimes against the legislative power;
- Of crimes against public justice;
- Of crimes against the person;
- Of crimes against the person involving sexual assault, and crimes against public decency and good morals;
- Of crimes against religion and conscience, and other offenses against good morals;
- Of crimes against public health and safety;
- Of crimes against the public peace;
- Of crimes against the revenue and property of this state;
- Of crimes against property;
- Malicious mischief;
- Miscellaneous crimes.

In this book, when discussing some of the criminal conducts existing, we are focusing on crimes regarding titles 8 and 9 – of crimes against the person and the ones against the person involving sexual assault, and crimes against public decency and good morals – and title 13, of crimes against property.

According to the code's title one, "the persons liable to punishment for crimes", all persons are capable of committing crimes, except: children under the age of 14, idiots, the one's who acted in ignorance or mistaken of fact, disproved the intent, people who were unconscious when acted, people who acted accidently, when there was no evil design, intention, or culpable negligence. (Section 25-29, 26).

Regarding the young between 14 and 21, they commit crimes, but are tried in juvenile courts, instead of adult courts. The age to be tried as adults vary from state to state, between 14 and 21.

As to the parties to a crime, they are classified in **principals** and **accessories.** Principles are the ones who directly acted, aid and abet the crime commission, or, not being present, advised or encourage its commission or still the ones who "by threats, menaces, command, or coercion, compel another to commit any crime" (California Legislative Information, 2021. Section 30-33, 31). The ones who in anyway help a felon, with the intention that the principal avoid the justice criminal system, is an accessory.

Crime is defined by law as a public offense, that is, an act, committed or omitted, in violation to the law that prohibits it or demands it, to which a sanction is applicable. That meaning, a crime can be the action of a prohibited conduct or the omission of a demanded one, if that is established by law. Legality principle is valid in that system.

The criminal sanctions present in the penal code are death, imprisonment, removal from office or disqualification to hold and enjoy any office of honor, trust, or profit in the State (Section 2-24, 15, CPC). Criminal conducts are classified as felonies, misdemeanors and infractions.

CPC–Section 2-24

16. Crimes and public offenses include:

1. Felonies;

2. Misdemeanors; and

3. Infractions.

17. (a) A felony is a crime which is punishable with death or by imprisonment in the state prison. Every other crime or public offense is a misdemeanor except those offenses that are classified as infractions.(California Legislative Information, 2021)

Felonies are considered more serious crimes, penalized with death or imprisonment – of a year or more. As to misdemeanors, they are considered less serious crimes, usually penalized with fines or imprisonment for less than a year. We will discuss crimes belonging to both species.

Besides the criminal sanctions listed, many states embraced the ideal of applying intermediate sanctions, through what is called "community based sanctions". That is a group of alternative penalties, which objectives are reducing prison population in addition to providing opportunities for the criminal's behavioral change (California Public Policy Institute, 2015).

The rational behind that policy is the idea that incarceration impoverishes and diminishes the individual's potential in life, also affecting the individual's family. Social reinsertion, due to stigmatization and conviction's collateral effects, can be very hard, what implicates in a extreme difficulty in living and working (Tonry, 2017, p. 190). Besides that, prison overpopulation also has an impact in the adoption of alternative sanction policies.

The measures are designated to those who were convicted of non-violent crimes, whose criminal sanctions are diminished. They are applied by both public and private correctional agencies, including, among others:

- Flash incarceration, for periods of less than 60 days;
- Intensive supervision;
- Home detention;
- Community services;
- Compulsory attendance to professional or educational programs;
- Drug use treatment;
- Random drug testing.

Generally, alternative measures to imprisonment are not plausible regarding sexual crimes or violent criminal conducts (CPC, part 3, title 9, chapter 2, article 1 [general previsions, 850-8052]).

As to the crime elements, the CPC, in article 20, defines that for a conduct to be considered a crime, there must be present the intent or, at least, criminal negligence.

> CPC: "20. In every crime or public offense there must exist a union, or joint operation of act and intent, or criminal negligence".

There is what is called specific intention crimes, that meaning, criminal conducts which demand a specific state of mind of its perpetrator in order for them to be characterized. In those cases, in addition to committing an act that is against the law, it is required a specific subjective condition. The specific intention requirement is usually indicated in the statute by the words *intentionally, knowingly, purposely* and *willfully*. Burglary and murder (as an intended homicide) are examples of specific intended crimes.

Legal Vocabulary Bank

- **Burglary** – "2. The modern statutory offense of breaking and entering any building – not just a dwelling, and not only at night – with the intent to commit a felony". Black Law's Dictionary, 2011, p. 91). The individual's specific intention when entering someone's property may vary, from stealing objects to raping the person who finds herself in the premises.
- **Murder** – "The killing of a human being with malice aforethought". (Garner, 2016, p. 500).

If specific intent crimes require a specific mental state of the individual, general intent crimes, on the other hand, only require the conduct realization to be characterized. The perpetrator's intent or specific state of mind regarding causing damages or obtaining determined result is not relevant. The only thing that needs to be proved is the intention of performing the prohibited conduct.

Driving under the influence of toxic substances and second-degree murder are examples of general intent crimes. If a person drinks and drives, no matter she has no intention of causing damages – and she actually does not need to cause any damages, she has performed a prohibited conduct, thus, she has committed a crime.

There are also situations relative to transferred intent, in which the criminal act reaches a different results than the ones intended. The individual's culpability in those cases rest in the rational that *"the intent follows the bullet"*. So, for example, if A wanted to kill B, killing C instead, A answers criminally for the murder of C. This is exactly the rational behind the felony murder, which will be discussed when we talk about some criminal conducts.

Differently from criminal intent, criminal negligence is an inferior degree of culpability, applied to crimes which results were not intended by the individual. It is understood that, in those cases, the perpetrator of the conduct acted recklessly. The rationales behind it relate to the despair of human life and the absence of reasonable care, regarding a reasonable person standard. Negligent conducts encompass situations where the person simply did not foresee the risk of her conduct or, foreseeing it, did not believe the results would actually happen.

The criminal statutes also make differences regarding attempted crimes, those being crimes that are not fully perpetrated due to the individual's inefficiency or due to third parties interception.

> **664 PC** "every person who attempts to commit any crime, but fails, or is prevented or intercepted in its perpetration [is guilty of a crime]...".

When the attempt is characterized the statute estimates a penalty reduction, in 50%. As to criminal responsibility, young offenders are subjected to juvenile courts, although the age to be tried as an adult varies within the states – from 14 to 21 years. However, in the past years there has been a generalized move towards the elevation of the criminal responsibility age[1]. Despite that, states count on the transfer of juveniles to adult courts, mechanism that enable juveniles to be tried as adults. One of the options that make that possible is the statutory exclusion, which determines certain crimes that when committed by young defendants allow their trial by adult courts.

This transfer to adult courts can also take place upon the prosecution's request, in cases of hybrid jurisdiction crimes – criminal conducts susceptible to both juvenile and adult courts. The decision regarding the trying court remains with the

---

1 For more see: <https://www.nytimes.com/roomfordebate/2015/12/14/what-age-should-young-criminals-be-tried-as-adults/raise-the-minimum-age-a-juvenile-can-be-tried-as-an-adult-to-21.>.

prosecution. Finally, if the minor has a history in the criminal justice, that being, if an adult court had already tried the defendant, in case of future trials he will be tried as an adult (National Conference of State Legislatures, 2021).

To conclude our reflections regarding some aspects of the general part of American criminal statutes, giving emphasis to the Californian Penal Code, it is interesting to discuss some common criminal defense's arguments.

In an attempted crime, for example, one of the arguments regarding the perpetrator's defense relates to abandonment, when the defendant completely and voluntarily desists from the original criminal purpose – not all jurisdictions recognize abandonment. However, statutes, which contemplate the institute, address it as an inchoate offense, that must not be confused with an intended rime. It includes acts that, in anyway, contributes towards a crime commission, such as "enticing, lying in wait for, or following the intended victim or unlawfully entering a building where a crime is expected to be committed. Model Penal Code, 5.01." (Garner, 2016, p. 55).

In negligent crime cases, the defense arguments relate to errors made by the individual, accidents that might have taken place, the lack of knowledge regarding prohibitions or that the criminal result occurred despite the individual's reasonable care.

As to intended crimes there are justificatory and exculpatory situations. Justifications relates to the fact the act or omission had a reason for existing. That reason must be sufficient to deconstitute the criminal offense – self-defense is an example of justification. An imperfect justification relates to an insufficient reason to justify the defendant's conduct, but can be used in court to mitigate the criminal sanction (Garner, 2016, p. 427).

Excuses relate to the fact that, despite acting in a way that would make him be considered a criminal, the defendant is not blameworthy. Traditional excuses encompass the following defenses: duress, entrapment, infancy, insanity and involuntary intoxication (Garner, 2016, p. 287).

Duress relates to the act of compelling someone to act against his will by threatening him of harm. Entrapment means inducement or undo persuasion – it has to be proved that the defendant would not have committed the crime otherwise. Infancy relates to the defendant's minority.

The American Criminal statutes, despite differing within states, present many similarities. The reason for that, in the first place, is that the US Constitution is originated from the one established within the 13 colonies, inspired by the British common law system.

In addition to that, the 14th Amendment, which implements the due process of law in the American system, has submitted all states to this criminal procedure principle. Both of these facts bring certain uniformity to the legal system (Bisharat, 2014, p. 769). Besides that, the modal penal code, and its general principles observation by the states' codes, also contributes at some degree to the uniformity among the nation's criminal laws.

Legal Vocabulary Bank

- **Aid and abet** – "To assist or facilitate the commission of a crime, or to promote its accomplishment. * Aiding and abetting is a crime in most jurisdictions. – aider and abettor, *n.*" (Garner, 2016, p. 30).
- **Criminal negligence** – "Gross negligence so extreme that it is punishable as a crime". Negligence: "The failure to exercise the standard of care that a reasonably prudent person would have exercised in a similar situation" (Garner, 2016, p. 509).
- **Criminal intent** – "1. Mens rea. 2. An intent to commit an actus reus without any justification, excuse, or other defense." Intent: "The state of mind accompanying an act, esp. a forbidden act. While motive is the inducement to do some act, intent is the mental resolution or determination to do it" (Garner, 2016, p. 395). Intentionally, *adv.*
- **Malice aforethought** – "The requisite mental state for common-law murder, encompassing anyone of the following: (1) the intent to kill, (2) the intent to inflict any grievous bodily harm, (3) extremely reckless indifference to the value of human life (the so-called "abandoned and malignant heart"), or (4) the intent to commit a dangerous felony (which leads to culpability under the felony-murder).
- **Specific intention** – "The intent to accomplish the precise criminal act that one is later charged with" (Garner, 2016, p. 396).

- **Knowingly** – "Deliberate, conscious way" (Garner, 2016, p. 429). In a deliberated way.
- **Willfully** – Voluntarily and intentionally, but not necessarily maliciously (Garner, 2016, p. 830).
- **Abandonment** – "Criminal law: Renunciation" (Garner, 2016, p. 1). Attempted crime defense argument.
- **Entice** – "To lure or induce; esp., to wrongfully solicit (a person) to do something – enticement, *n*. (Garner, 2016, p. 268).
- **Blame** – "1. An act of attributing fault; an expression of disapproval. 2. Responsibility for something wrong. Blameworthy, *adj*" (Garner, 2016, p. 79).
- **Inchoate [offense]** – "adj. Partially completed or imperfectly formed; just begun." (Garner, 2016, p. 371). Attempted crime – inchoate offense.
- **Mistake of fact** – "2. The defense asserting that a criminal defendant acted from an innocent misunderstanding of fact rather than from a criminal purpose" (Garner, 2016, p. 490).
- **Mistake of law** – "2. The defense asserting that a defendant did not understand the criminal consequences of a certain conduct. * This defense is not as effective as a mistake of fact." (Garner, 2016, p. 490).
- **Motive** – "Something, esp. willful desire, that leads one to act." (Garner, 2016, p. 499).

— 4.1.2 —
Types of Crime

We have gotten to the point where it is interesting to discuss some types of crime in the US criminal statutes, analyzing some of its characteristics. As we have had the opportunity to observe before, the criminal laws in America hold some very specific particularities, such as the "wobbler" offenses and the "three strikes" law.

That is also true regarding crime classification. The common criminal conduct of killing someone can also hold unique particularities in the American criminal law, as we are going to see ahead. As the reader is going to notice, we are giving preference to the analysis of a few personal and property crimes.

The act of killing someone, a homicide, is considered a very serious offense. However, the degree in which this conduct is reprehensible will depend on the offender's intention and his state of mind when acting. Therefore, the crime has different classifications, which may also vary according to the jurisdiction.

Generally there is first and second-degree murder and voluntary manslaughter. In some jurisdictions it is present the offense of felony murder – which has been excluded from the Model Penal Code.

According to the California Penal Code, the offense is classified as:

> Art. 187 CP, murder: "the unlawful killing of a human being or fetus with malice aforethought."

For first-degree murder a specific intent must be present in the offender's conduct, which is designated as "malice aforethought". That means the offender must have had that state of mind, as a requisite to the intended murder offense, which may be understood as an intention to kill, to cause serious bodily harm or even a demonstration of great disregard to human life.

According to the Black Law's Dictionary (Garner, 2016, p. 500) definition, first-degree murder consists in:

> "(1895) Murder that is willful, deliberate, or premeditated [...]"

It is interesting to observe the words that indicate specific intent – as we have discussed previously – are present, those being, in this case, "willful, deliberated, and premeditated". The Californian Law also understands as intended murder the acts that used mass destruction weapons, such as bombs.

As to second-degree murder offenses, these are comprehended as acts which do not encompass the intention of killing another person (CPC, art. 189). It encompasses cases of criminal negligence or cases where the killing took place in the course of the commission of a crime that would not originate a felony murder. A few states have added to their statutes a third-degree murder, but most jurisdictions classify murder only in first or second-degree. A third-degree murder would be defined as "a wrong that did not constitute murder at common law" (Garner, 2016, p. 501).

Manslaughter is not a degree of the crime a murder but a different offense instead, that being, the unlawful killing of person, but without malice aforethought. In the voluntary manslaughter the offender, in the heat of the moment, with no previous intent of committing the crime, acts, killing another person. It resumes to "an act of murder reduced to manslaughter because of extenuating circumstances such as adequate provocation (arousing the "heat of passion") or diminished capacity (Garner, 2016, p. 474).

The importance of the conduct classification matters in the concrete cases, once the criminal sanctions vary a lot depending on what crime is the accused charged with. For first-degree murder criminal sanctions go from 25 years to life in prison, to death penalty – in some states.

For second-degree murder, the criminal sentence may determine imprisonment from 15 years to life.

> CPC 190 a) Every person guilty of murder in the first degree shall be punished by death, imprisonment in the state prison for life without the possibility of parole, or imprisonment in the state prison for a term of 25 years to life. [...]
>
> [...] every person guilty of murder in the second degree shall be punished by imprisonment in the state prison for a term of 15 years to life.

As to voluntary manslaughter, penalties may vary from 3 to 11 years of imprisonment. (CPC, art. 193). Finally, to end the discussion regarding homicide, it is necessary to discuss the felony murder classification, present in many criminal statutes, despite its exclusion from the Model Penal Code.

The felony murder concept contemplates the following: "Felony-murder rule. (1943) The doctrine holding that any death resulting from the commission or attempted commission of a felony is a murder" (Garner, 2016, p. 311). The first-degree murder concept also embraces the act "that is committed during the course of another dangerous felony" (Garner, 2016, p. 500).

As clearly observed, that rule broadens the murder one, once if an offender kills while committing a distinct crime (a felony), he and the other participants in the felony may be accused of first degree murder (felony murder) regardless of the intention to kill or the offender's state of mind.

For example, if two individuals enter a pharmacy to rob it, and one of them accidentally shoots and kills the store's cashier, both offenders may be charged with first-degree murder under the felony murder rule. That is possible even if the offenders had proved to not have the intention of killing the cashier. The rule is based in the transferred intent theory. "Transferred intent and the felony murder rule have a common origin, the early common law treating the two as the same thing–a technique for finding the implied malice on which a conviction of murder could be based" (Wilfred, 1959, p. 170).

The doctrine, or fiction, discussed serves as the basis for imposing criminal liability and the rule, in most jurisdictions, applies to felonies, which are considered dangerous to human life, such as rape, robbery and burglary, encompassing acts in which it is foreseeable some possibility of causing harm to others. However, not all jurisdictions adopt the felony-murder fiction.

Another crime classification that is very interesting to analyze is rape, due to both, its characteristics and criminal consequences. There are many types of rape in the American criminal law, figuring among them the common rape and marital rape. In these circumstances the sexual intercourse happens with the use of force, coercion or violence, that meaning, without the victim's consent, what may also happen due to intoxication or somnolence. (CPC, art. 261). Sexual assault regards an unwanted sexual contact, without penetration.

As to the statutory rape, it is characterized whenever the victim is underage to give consent – in California that age is 18. However, according to that statute, if the age difference between the parties is no higher than 3 years, the crime can be considered a misdemeanor. On the other hand, if the accused is over 21 and the victim is younger than 16, the crime is considered a felony, and the sentence given may be up to 4 years of imprisonment (CPC, art. 261.5).

At this moment some observations relating to the collateral consequences surrounding the crime of rape are essential. First, it should be noted that in a great number of prisons and jails, sexual offenders are incarcerated in a different wing, also being differentiated by uniform colors – in the Los Angeles County

Jail, for example, regular inmates use orange and those known as sexual predators, use red.

Furthermore, once a person has a conviction for a sexual offense, she is registered in a national sex offender registry, which is maintained by the justice department of each jurisdiction and is available to the community, online. In California that is acknowledged as the "Megan's Law"[12].

Such register also exerts limitations on the offender, such as geographic ones regarding housing and working locations. Usually, former sexual offenders may not live near areas where there is great circulation of kids, such as schools.

Studies point that these collateral consequences of the conviction, considered administrative punishment, is a greater sanction than the penal one, served by the convict. The community announcement on the ex-convict freedom and his current address reaches not only the ex-offender but also his family.

In those cases it is determined a great family financial loss, added to a great difficulty in finding a job, besides a high rate of housing contract's breach on the landlord's part or due to the impossibility of the tenant in paying rent. Social isolation takes place in the families' life, and frequently the ex-offender finds

---

2 "This website provides information on registered sex offenders pursuant to California Penal Code § 290.46 so that members of the public can better protect themselves and their families. The information on this site is extracted from the California Sex and Arson Registry (CSAR), the State's repository for sex offender information. The information in the CSAR is provided to local law enforcement agencies by the sex offender during the registration process." Available at: <https://www.meganslaw.ca.gov/>.

difficulties in exerting its parenting responsibilities, as giving school support to underage children.

Among the most common consequences faced by a sexual offense convict, when released from jail, is his stigmatization, the harassment suffered from general population and law enforcement agents and the sense of vulnerability (Frenzel et al., 2014, p. 4). It is necessary to highlight that studies show the policy adopted is not efficient on preventing sexual offenses.

The reason for that is the underreporting phenomenon. Most abuses are perpetrated by family members or friends of the victims, what makes the abused not to report the crime to the authorities, therefore, the offender is neither investigated nor tried, staying out of the sex offender registry.

After the observation relating to the rape types, we are moving our discussion to some of the existing crimes against property in the American statutes. Crimes against the property relate to the perturbation of one's right to use their property. Here we are covering the conducts characterized as theft, robbery, burglary and arson.

Theft is one of the most common crimes in the US jurisdiction and its designation may vary according to the state, also being acknowledged as larceny or petty theft, for example. According to the Black Law's Dictionary, theft is "broadly an act or instance of stealing, including larceny, burglary [...]. Many modern penal codes have consolidated such property offenses under the name "theft" (Garner, 2016, p. 755).

According to the legal dictionary, when defining larceny, the conduct is described as "Larceny: the unlawful taking and carrying away of someone else's personal property with the intent to deprive the possessor of it permanently" (Garner, 2016, p. 434).

Going further on the act of taking someone's property, the crime of robbery, also known as "theft by force" or aggravated larceny, has added to its elements the violence requisite. This crimes is considered a felony in most jurisdictions, however, some statutes may classify them as high misdemeanors. "Robbery: The illegal taking of property from the person of another, or in the person's presence, by violence or intimidation; [...]" (Garner, 2016, p. 661).

The use of a dangerous weapon (armed robbery) or the infliction of bodily harm on the victim may characterize aggravated robbery. It is usually an aggravating factor the victim to be children or the elderly.

The crime of burglary is also derived from theft, and we have talked a bit about it when we discussed the specific intended crimes. The crime is constituted by the act of invading someone else's property with the intention of committing felony – to rob the place, to rape the person who is in the premises, or other.

In California, the crime is regulated by the state's penal code, article 459 (CPC, 2021):

"every person who enters any house, room, apartment, tenement, shop, warehouse, store, mill, barn, stable, outhouse or other building, tent, vessel...with intent to commit grand or petit larceny or any felony is guilty of burglary."

Some statutes, instead of requiring the intent of committing a felony to characterize the burglary crime, make petit larceny an alterative in order to prove the accused's burglarious intent.

In California the crime is classified in first and second-degree. First-degree burglaries encompass situations regarding homes – in which cases the criminal sanction is stipulated between 2 to 6 years of imprisonment. As to the second-degree of the offense, it regards cases involving commercial buildings, and they can be considered felonies – 16 months to 3 years off imprisonment – or misdemeanors – 1 year of imprisonment, under the wobbler policy.

Also, in many statutes, to posses a tool supposedly designed to facilitate the invasion of someone's property (a burglary tool), is a crime, if proved the individual's intent to commit a burglary. (Garner, 2016, p. 91).

To finish the analysis of some of the felony crimes existing in the US criminal law, we brought the concept of the criminal conduct known as *arson*. Regarding common law concepts, that would be the conduct of burning someone's house or outhouse. Modernly, the classification of arson regards burning intentionally someone's property. The conduct can be aggravated if the arsonist knows someone will be in the burning property.

— 4.1.3 —
Misdemeanors

Misdemeanors are considered less serious offenses in the US criminal laws, as already stated. The criminal sanctions in theses cases are, generally, inferior to one year of imprisonment.

In California, all crimes that are not explicit felonies by the statute are considered misdemeanors, such as the statutory rape example given before – when the age difference between the involved is no higher than three years – or the conduct of driving under the influence (DUI). However, in that particular jurisdiction, as we have already discussed, there is the current wobbler policy, under which some crimes may be considered both, felonies or misdemeanors.

The misdemeanor policy in the US laws in surrounded by critics. Professor Alexandra Natapoff, from Loyola Law School, has conducted a study regarding overcriminalization of conducts under that policy, analyzing its effects on the American population and the country's criminal system.

According to the professor, most Americans who have been submitted to the criminal justice system, have been so through the misdemeanor law's application – that meaning, most criminal accused in the country have been persecuted due to less serious crimes, penalized with less than one year of imprisonment.

Numbers show 10 million cases of misdemeanors being criminally persecuted a year, representing 80% of all criminal cases in that system (Natapoff, 2012, p. 8). Statistics also point to the fact that only 5% of criminal detentions relate to serious crimes – felonies – according to the FBI's definitions, those being: homicide, rape and aggravated assault (ACLU, 2020).

Misdemeanors are not always sanctioned with prison or jail time, also being applied to those conducts alternative sanctions, which implicate in many obligations to the offender, such as the obligation of being employed, intense supervision and constant monitoring, random drug testing, among others – these obligations figure between what is called collateral *consequences of a criminal conviction.*

It is argued that the overcriminalization of human conducts is aimed to strike minorities, pulling them into the criminal justice system. Marijuana use, driving with an expired driver's license, taking two sits on the subway, truancy, are all examples of criminalized conducts in many jurisdictions under the misdemeanor policy. According to Natapoff (2012), this criminalized conducts are used as an excuse to supervise and monitor portions of the American population.

Goffman (2014), after months of research, following people's lives in Black communities in Chicago, describes how the system is entangled to convict poor and black people and how difficult it is for these population to get out of the criminal justice system.

Waquant (2011), Dieter (2013) and Natapoff (2012, p. 7) also corroborate the phenomenon, stating that minority' neighborhoods are submitted to more surveillance and police stops that are rare in upper class communities. African Americans are eight times more likely to be arrested by recreational use of marijuana; even citizens from all races use the substance in the same proportions (Natapoff, 2012, p. 22).

In addition to that, since many misdemeanors do not foresee incarceration, in those cases the criminal defense right does not attach, and is not offered to many of the accused. Therefore, even without the prevision of incarceration, many supposedly offenders end up being arrested, illegally, on account of pre-trial detention, under the impossibility of posting bail or due to the impossibility of paying the costs of the proceedings, as will discussed later (Natapoff, 2012, p. 29).

Moreover, it is proved that the accused's confession regarding misdemeanors during plea bargaining negotiations are responsible for the majority of judicial errors in the criminal system. There is a great amount of false confessions that take place due to the pressure exerted by the prosecution over the accused during the negotiation.

Decriminalization, such as in the case of misdemeanors, unlike fully legalization, preserves punitive features and collateral effects of the minor offense committed. "It actually expands the reach of the criminal apparatus by making it easier to impose fines and supervision on an ever-winding population [...]" (Natapoff, 2012).

By the analysis of the author's research it is arguable that the partial decriminalization's policies, in the way they are being implemented, only expanded the law enforcement's power over the people in a discretionary way, making it easier to push them into the criminal system.

Legal Vocabulary Bank

- **Initial appearance** – "A criminal defendant's first appearance in court to hear the charges read, to be advised of his or her rights, and to have bail determined. * The initial appearing is usu. Required by statute to occur without undue delay. In a misdemeanor case, the initial appearance may be combined with the arraignment" (Garner, 2016, p. 42).
- **Bail** – "A security such as cash or a bond; esp. security required by a court for the release of a prisoner who must appear in court at a future time <bail is set at US XX>" (Garner, 2016, p. 62).
- **To post bail** – "1. To obtain the release of (oneself or another) by providing security for a future appearance in court" (Garner, 2016, p. 62).
- **Excessive bail** – "Bail that is unreasonably high considering both the offense with which the accused is charged and the risk that the accused will not appear in trial. * The Eighth Amendment prohibits excessive bail" (Garner, 2016, p. 62).

- **Bail revocation** – "(1950) The court's cancellation of bail previously granted to a criminal defendant" (Garner, 2016, p. 63).
- **Pre-trial detention** – "(1962) 1. The holding of a defendant before trial on criminal charges either because the established bail could not be posted or because release was denied. [...]" (Garner, 2016, p. 228).
- **Truancy** – "The act or state of shirking responsibility; esp., willful and unjustified failure to attend school by one who is required to attend – truant, *adj. & n.*" (Garner, 2016, p. 777).

— 4.2 —

Introduction to criminal procedure: pre-trial process

Once we have had a glance at important points of the criminal laws in the US, we are now dedicating ourselves to examine the basic steps of the American criminal procedure. It is important to state that criminal procedure rules may vary from State to State. This is the reason why, due to pedagogical matters, we are working here with the Federal Criminal Procedure Rules. Regarding the rules that govern the criminal procedure and evidence, each state has similar rules.

The laws that govern how criminal prosecutions are conducted on a federal level are organized in the Federal Rules of Criminal Procedure and the rules that govern the admissibility and use of evidence in criminal proceedings are available at Federal Rules of Evidence.

The proceedings are divided into two phases; the first one encompasses pre-trial proceedings, as the second one relates to the trial proceedings. We are starting our analysis with the pre-trial phase.

This phase comprehends the investigation, the initial hearing and arraignment, discovery, plea bargaining and preliminary hearing also giving space to pre-trial motions.

The investigative activity is done by law enforcement agents – in the state sphere the competent police department and in a federal sphere, by federal agencies such as the Federal Bureau of Investigation (FBI), the Drug Enforcement Administration (DEA), the United States Secret Services (USSS) and Homeland Security investigation.

Regarding criminal offenses, the prosecutor is the representative of the state and he is responsible for all criminal cases' decisions that may be presented judicially. During the investigative preceding the prosecution also plays important parts providing support to the police as to the evidence required for conviction in the investigating case, also providing investigative tools to the police, such as search or arrest warrants. With that in mind, it is important to notice that the prosecutor must enforce the lawfulness of the investigation. (Heymann and Petrie, 2001, pg. 8).

In a general matter, the investigation usually involves a search warrant, as we have already seen, that should be issued by a neutral judge. The reason for that is the stated in the 4th Amendment, which protects people from unreasonable searches and seizures. The warrant requirement is probable cause, that meaning, to issue an warrant a judge must be convinced that there is reasonable believe, based on the circumstances, that a crime had occurred or is about to (Carroll v. United States 267, U.S. 132, 149, 925).

If a person or a person's object is searched or seizure without a warrant, the evidence obtained through that unlawful activity is considered illegal and under the exclusionary rule it must be suppressed (Mapp v. Ohio 367 U.S. 643, 1961).

As we have also discussed before, there are exceptions to the warrant requirement, therefore, in some situations law enforcement officials can waive a warrant. The exceptions to warrant requirements are:

- Exigent Circumstances – Fernandez v. California (2014)
- Consent to Search – Chimmel v. California (1969)
- Search Incident to Lawful Arrest – Riley v. California (2014)
- Automobile Exception – Arizona v. Gant (2009)
- Plain View and Open Field Exception – Oliver v. United Stated (1984)
- Terry Stops – Terry v. Ohio (1968)
- Border Searchers – United States v. Montoya de Hernandes (1985)

> For further development on the subject see: Chemerinski, Erwin. Levenson, Laurie L. "Criminal Procedure: Investigation (Aspen Casebook Series, 2018)".

After a defendant is arrested an initial appearance is held, and this is the moment the defendant knows what he is being accused of and has the chance to give his version of the facts. Also, this is the time arrangements are made so the defendant has access to a defense attorney, when it is the case. The judge decides then if the accused may be released or should remain in custody. If the requirements are met, the accused may be released under bail. If there is the need, due to the impossibility of the accused in posting bail or if the bail amount should be revised, a bail hearing may be held.

The procedure starts with the criminal investigation, moves to the initial appearance. Than if the defendant pleas not guilty a preliminary hearing is held. It has to occur in until 14 days since the initial appearance – if the accused is placed in jail, or 21 days if he is otherwise out, on bail. Its purpose is to establish probable cause that the defendant actually committed the crime, what has to be demonstrated by the accusation, since the burden of proof in on the prosecution. If the judge is convinced by the accusation that the accused may be prosecuted, the accused will be indicted, and trial will be scheduled. As we will see ahead, since the investigative phase it is possible to negotiate with the prosecution a guilty plea, through the plea-bargaining proceeding.

The next step is discovery, in order to reveal facts and develop evidence. This is when both parties, accusation and defense, prepare themselves to trial – gathering information on the case, seeking for evidence and talking to witnesses, including the ones who could be called to testify in court.

The rational behind the practice is also to "prevent the parties from surprising each other with evidence at trial" (Garner, 2011, p. 236). That is very clear under the Brady Rule, which obliges the prosecution to disclose to the accused any exculpatory information gathered (Brady v. Maryland, 1963).

Brady participated in a robbery, joined by Boblit, in which a person was killed. A jury found both the offenders guilty of first-degree murder. Brady stated he had only participated on the robbery, not the killing. Both men were sentenced to death. After trial it was revealed that Boblit had confessed the murder and the prosecution did not share that exculpatory evidence with Brady's defense.

On appeal it was decided that the suppression of Boblit's confession denied Brady due process. The legal issue raised by the case was weather the prosecution's suppression of Boblit's confession denied Brady due process. The circuit court's holding was that he prosecution's suppression of evidence violated the Due Process Clause of the Fourteenth Amendment.

Just as a general comment, the procedural rules allow a scope of discovery (Federal Rules of Evidence, rule 16 – Discovery and Inspection), which should not be expanded (Norton, 1970). However, there are attempts to elicit information from the other party that go beyond the allowed practice, this technique is known as *fishing expedition*.

Finally, during the pre-trial phase motions are an option in order to guarantee the observation of all the procedure and evidence rules. This are called pre-trial motions and may regard the evidence, the discovery phase, the defendant, the courtroom, among others.

Ahead, we listed some of the possible pre-trial motions (Garner, 2012, p. 498), many of them related to the pre-trial steps analyzed before:

- **Motion in limine** – A request for inadmissible evidence not be referred or offered at trial. When evidence is considered highly prejudicial, even if only mentioned in court, not being sufficient the request for the jury disregard it. If after granted the motion, the other party mentions the forbidden evidence, a mistrial may be ordered.
- **Motion to compel discovery** – A request so the other party respond to its opponent's discovery request.
- **Motion to suppress** – A request for the court to prohibit the use of illegally obtained evidence.
- **Motion to dismiss** – In case of settlement or procedural defect a request to dismiss the case may be made to the court.

- **Motion to transfer venue** – Transfer the case to another district under the allegation that the original venue is improper – due to pre-trial publicity, for example).
- **Motion to withdraw** – A request that the attorney cease representing his client.

We would like now, before analyzing aspects of the trial phase, to discuss the already mentioned plea-bargaining proceeding, which usually takes place in the pre-trial phase.

Legal Vocabulary Bank

- **Criminal charge** – "A formal accusation of an offense as a preliminary step to prosecution" (Garner, 2016, p. 108).
- **Indictment** – "The formal written accusation of a crime, made by a grand jury and presented to a court for prosecution against the accused person" (Garner, 2016, p. 377).
- **Due process** – "The conduct of legal proceedings according to established rules and principles for the protection and enforcement of private rights, including notice and the right to a fair hearing before a tribunal with the power to decide the case" (Garner, 2016, p. 253).
- **Fishing Expedition** – "An attempt, through broad discovery requests or random questions, to elicit information from another party in the hope that something relevant might

> be found; esp., such an attempt that exceeds the scope of discovery allowed by procedural rules" (Garner, 2016, p. 315).
> - **Mistrial** – "1. A trial that the judge brings to an end, without a determination on the merits, because of a procedural error or serious misconduct occurring during the proceedings. 2. A trial that ends inconclusively because the jury cannot agree on a verdict" (Garner, 2016, p. 491).

— 4.3 —
Plea bargaining

Putting it simple, the plea bargaining police consists in the possibility of pleading a deal to avoid trial, sometimes reducing the time to be spent in jail. It is a negotiation between prosecution and defense. In the US 95% of criminal cases are solved through the plea bargaining system. It is a very criticized institute since its design and (lack of) regulation open space for injustices, as we are going to analyze in details, below, based on a previous research done by the author (Kalache, 2020).

The Plea Bargaining System as practiced in the US has overvalued efficiency – in a degree that the justice system has become a hostage of the practice – to the detriment of basic constitutional and human rights, in hence serving to maintain the status quo regarding the not declared purposes of punishment – criminal selectivity.

Among the major issues involving the negotiation, at this moment we are giving emphasis to the failure to observe constitutional basic rights, such as the due process of law and the presumption of innocence, resulting from the accusatory practices, leading to the persecution of minorities.

Effectiveness above legality – critics on the prosecution's practices

To start, it is elementary to know that 95%[13] of criminal cases in North America are sentenced through the plea bargaining system. No courtroom, no jury, no due process, and in many cases not even a defense attorney present. Instead, a small room, sitting, in one side of the table, the prosecution, in the other the accused, negotiating the accused's destiny, based on the evidence the prosecution decides to share – or to intimidate the accused with – dealing in a speedy and lest costly way with the supposedly "law breakers" in America. Incarcerating human beings and/or restricting people's rights have definitely become less burdensome.

Plea Bargaining has become the dominant force of the American criminal procedure. "That power derived ultimately from the individual power from those whose interests plea bargaining served" (Fisher, 2003, p. 1). Based on this information only, it is not hard to comprehend how prison population in

---

3 The Kings of the Courtroom – How Prosecutors came to Dominate the Criminal Justice System. THE ECONOMIST. Available at: <https://www.economist.com/news/united-states/21621799-how-prosecutors-came-dominate-criminal-justice-system-kings-courtroom>. Access in February, 6th, 2019.

North America has exploded, achieving the notorious mark of 2.2 million Americans incarcerated by 2012, the largest number in the whole world, what raises questions about the fairness of the procedure.

To understand how unfair it turns to be, below it is analyzed what are the controversial points taken in consideration by the prosecution when selecting the cases granted with a plea deal and under what conditions. Then, it is discussed the role of the prosecution and the excessive power granted to them, annihilating the point of balance between defense and accusation forces. It was also the intention to remark evidence problems in the negotiations, emphasizing critics to the not requirement of robust evidence at the negotiation moment, evidence disclosure and the use of unconstitutional evidence. Finally it is analyzed the impact of plea deals on criminal selectivity and the consequent incarceration of the poor.

Seeking a speedy solution

There is no discussion regarding the fact that negotiating a criminal case is speedy and less costly then sending it to trial. It is estimated that if ten percent of the criminal cases in Manhattan went to trial, the system would break – today, less than five percent of cases are tried in courts. Speed is such a great component taken in consideration when dealing with cases that the longer the trial would be to determined case, the bigger the chances the prosecution offers a good plea deal. Moreover, signalizing long time in court – including asking to hear a great number of witnesses, for example – is a technique used by defense to cut a great deal for clients.

As an example it is possible to cite cases such as Bordenkircher v. Hayes (1978), in which the prosecution offered a plea deal of five years in prison "in order to save the court the inconvenience and necessity of a trial". Prosecutors, in general, agree that backlog of cases usually have a great impact in their decisions to offer a plea, but they are not the most important factor in motivating a bargaining decision. Viability to secure conviction in trial is.

When a conviction in trial is doubtful, prosecutors are more likely to offer a guilty plea. The rational behind the practice is simple: conviction rates instead of the adequate punishment. "When the case has a hole in it, however, the prosecutor may scale the offer all the way down to probation. The prosecutors' goal is to get something from every defendant, and the correctional treatment the defendant may require is the last thing on their minds" (Alschuler, 1968, p. 60).

As a natural consequence of this behavior are the cases where innocent people plea guilty, demonstrating a complete disregard by the criminal justice to the danger of false conviction.

> The practice of responding to a weak case by offering extraordinary concessions therefore represents, at best, a dangerous allocation of institutional responsibility. And when even the minimal safeguard of a prosecutorial judgment of guilt is lacking, as it is in a significant number of cases today,

the horrors of the guilty-plea system are multiplied. (Alschuler, 1968, p. 64)

It is clear that judicial and prosecutorial resources are not being conserved in the bargaining process when selecting the cases that should be offered a plea and under what conditions, as no sentence should be imposed to anyone whose guilt is uncertain, in order to favor a less expensive and faster resolution of the case. That is one of the critics made regarding the prosecution practice towards plea negotiations.

The multiple roles played by the accusation and its excessive power

Moreover, in order to accomplish the effectiveness goal, changes had to be made in relation to the prosecution role in the criminal cases. The prosecution discretionary power has been enlarged in order to enable pleas, since the prosecution goal is to secure a guilty plea and, in order to achieve this goal, concessions are supposedly granted in exchange.

Many critics raised questions as to the legality of the roles played by the prosecutor during the bargaining process, as he acts as a) an administrator – seeking to deal with the cases in a speedy and efficient way, b) an advocate – maximizing the conviction numbers and the severity of the sentences, c) a judge – deciding what is the correct deal to be given to each defendant, and d) a legislator – granting concessions based on the harshness of the law (Alschuler, 1968, p. 54). It seems clear to be excessive the power given to the prosecution during the plea negotiations – besides the critics on the judge's role on plea agreements, as there is the need for a neutral party to step into the procedure to assure its observation to the law, avoiding any abuse that may occur, what has no been practiced today.

Despite the optimism involving the system – from both, efficiency and monetary points of view – research has shown that it presents many inconsistencies and flaws, raising serious questions concerning its legality and fairness. The discretionary power in filling charges and overcharging are among the concerns being raised by many defense attorneys and scholars – in drug cases, for example, the accusation gets to decide how much of the product can be designated as the dealer's.

When analyzing the charging criteria, it seems that the guiding principle for charging among prosecutors is the "highest and the most" that the evidence permits. But this rationale is not sustained when accepting a guilty plea – when the counts go dramatically down. When accepting a guilty plea what seems to matter the most is the adequate scope for punishment. It is argued by some defense attorneys that in some jurisdictions the charge follows the criteria: "'the first degree of everything" but accept a guilty plea to' the second degree of any crime" without serious negotiation" (Alschuler, 1968, p. 90). It is possible to recognize the use of the charge in the bargain process as a toll in order to solve cases in a speedy as less costly manner, and its effect in the process is to avoid trial.

The third concern is about overcharging. Besides denied by the prosecution, claims of overcharging are present in almost every jurisdiction (Alschuler, 1968, p. 85). Defense attorneys characterize this practice "when the only reason for filling a charge is to induce a plea of guilty to some other charge" (Alschuler, 1968, p. 86). But it can also be understood as an offense charged at a higher level than the case seems to be.[14] This overcharging technique plays an important part, in addition to the over criminalization of conducts, when it comes to criminal selectivity, as discussed forward.

Prosecutors argue that this independency regarding the deals they choose and how they choose to offer them, is the reason why the proceeding is successful, being indispensable to make feasible the guilty pleas. The whole idea of the practice is to seek justice in a speedy and less costly manner and changing, or anyhow narrowing, the prosecution role would have a great impact on that.

The bargaining practice, in its actual terms, seems to go against to what is stated by the American Constitution, in its Fifth Amendment, that "No person shall be... deprived of life, liberty, or property, without due process of law...". What the document promised to assure to the American people was

---

4   " When an embezzler has made false entries in his employer's books over a long period of time, for example, it is not difficult for a prosecutor to prepare a fifty- or one-hundred-count indictment. And when a first-offender has passed a dozen bad checks, a prosecutor may file a dozen separate accusations." (Alschuler, 1968, p. 87)

that, the American government, in al its levels, would operate in accordance to the law, providing fair procedures.

Offering a plea based on the possibility of an acquittal if the case went to trial, or based on the prosecutor's workload, or even making it based on the "overcharging method" in order to push the accused to plea guilty, does not seem to be in accordance to the fair procedure constitutionally determined. And the same troubling rational is made by the prosecutors when it comes to the evidence admitted during the negotiations, that being massive incrimination, what leads to the next topic to be discussed.

Evidence problems

Evidence problems constitute another disconcerting factor in the plea deal dynamic. The accusation has broad discretion to determine how much evidence is sufficient in order to proceed with the case, and charging decisions are made when decisive evidence is not required yet – way before preparation for trial. Nonetheless, the blurry area is not restricted to the necessity of robust evidence during a negotiation. Constitutional issues are being raised against the evidence accepted during the procedure.

A study shows that 46%[15] of wrongful capital convictions were based on false testimony. As an example it is possible to

---

5   The Kings of the Courtroom – How Prosecutors came to Dominate the Criminal Justice System. THE ECONOMIST. Available at: <https://www.economist.com/news/united-states/21621799-how-prosecutors-came-dominate-criminal-justice-system-kings-courtroom>. Access on February, 6th, 2019.

name Cameron Todd Willingham's[16] case, in which the main evidence that guaranteed his conviction to death penalty was later proved to be manufactured in a false testimony, in return for efforts by the prosecution to secure reduced sentence. It is common for the prosecution to offer a deal to give benefits in exchange of co-operation, and the practice has been questioned as to the truthiness of the information due to the circumstances they were given.

But false testimony is not the only evidential illegality raised. (Mis)Identification of the accused is also a great deal. Identifications made with the suspects facing the wall – identification "from behind" – and several other flaws in the procedure, such as the use of polygraph on the suspect as a coercion method, have put in check the evidence used by the prosecution in many cases.

The culture of "not letting anyone go free" among accusation practitioners is so wildly spread and so strong that some prosecutors themselves suffer with it in some cases. Sonia Antolec[17] is a good example of that, having resigned after she was suspended for dropping a weak case with evidence problems.

As concluded by Alschuler, the system of plea bargain is currently dictated by prosecutors and resumes itself in secret

---

6   In this case the family of the accused was killed in a fire at their house. The accused was found in front of the house while it was in flames. Available at: <https://www.newyorker.com/magazine/2009/09/07/trial-by-fire>. Access on March 7th, 2019.

7   In this case the victims were asked to identify the suspects "from behind", with them facing the wall. Available at: <https://www.pressreader.com/usa/chicago-sun-times/20130807/281616713001574>. Access on March 1st 2019.

negotiations behind closed doors in the prosecutor's office, not being subjected to nearly no review, not even internally, neither by the courts. It is a one-sided system, and the prosecutor holds all the cards of the game when it comes to the evidence and the facts of the case itself. Under such unsustainable pressure allowed by the system, it appears to have led a great number of innocent defendants to plead guilty.

Analyzing the procedures surrounding plea negotiations, it could be argued that the due process clause, constitutionally imposed, has been threatened. The multiple parts played by the accusation, its excessive power in filling the charges and molding the plea deals, the overcharging technique to close plea deals and the illegality of many evidence used during the negotiation are in clear dissonance to the constitutional principle.

Plea Bargaining and its reflection on minorities

The process of convicting citizens to jail time has been reduced to a few minutes conversation, or persuasion, where prosecution threat leads the tone of the negotiation instead of the proved facts regarding the case. As a result to the practice, US faces an incarceration boom – that happened despite the fact that violent crimes have suffered a decrease of almost 50% (Taibbi, 2014, p. xvi). This "bizarre triangle", in Taibbi's words, is composed by three factors: poverty going up – around 15% by 2010 – crime rates going down and prison population going gigantic.

This information, in addition to prison population data[18] – which is composed, largely by African American and Hispanic people – leads to only one conclusion: the effectiveness brought by the American plea bargaining system is aligned with what the critical criminologists call "the undeclared purpose of punishment", meaning: the real purpose of excluding and neutralizing minorities.

Questions may be raised to this statement, as to how does the system promote criminal selectivity, once the negotiation is offered to all Americans who have allegedly committed crimes. Not entering in the analysis of the structure and specifics of the actuarial policy (see in Waquant, 2011, and Dieter, 2013) – which contributes a lot to this understanding, but takes a hole other paper to be discussed, the bargaining system itself guards some specifics that contributes to minority incarceration. As examples could be brought to light situations involving negotiations made without the assistance of a defense attorney,[19] or, in many cases where the defender was present the defense was ineffective. Also, can be brought to discussion the cases where pre-trial

---

8   While African-Americans are 12% of the total population, when it comes to prison population they represent 33% of the incarcerated. On the other hand, whites constitute 64% of the adults in the USA, but only 30% of them are in prison, according to the Bureau of Justice Statistics data. Correctional Populations in the United States, 2016 report. Available at: <https://www.bjs.gov/content/pub/pdf/cpus16.pdf>. Access on May, 3rd 2019.

9   With the costs related to criminal justice figuring among the fifth highest ones in the American government, and the mass campaign for cost savings in many governmental policies, to cut or at least to reduce funding indigent defense was a start point for trying to achieve these goals. Justice Denied: America's Continuing Neglect of Our Constitutional Right to Counsel, National Right to Counsel Committee (2009): 32-43.

detention was used to obtain a guilty plea from the defendant – low-income people are less likely to post bail, for reasons that do not need to be explained.

> It is entirely possible that most wrongful convictions – like 90 percent or more of all criminal convictions – are based on negotiated guilty pleas to comparatively light charges, and that the innocent defendants in those cases received little or no time in custody. If so, it may well be that a major cause of these comparatively low-level miscarriages of justice is the prospect of prolonged pretrial detention by innocent defendants who are unable to post bail. (Gross, 2008, p. 940)

Finally, among many other practices that subdue minorities in the criminal system, there is one that has direct consequences in the mass incarceration of the poor. Over criminalization of conducts, resulting in misdemeanors.

The country faces a legislative inflation and bad utilization of the criminal law, conceding to the State interference in many aspects of its citizens private lives, criminalizing behaviors taken as "preoccupying", enlarging the list of the people holding a criminal record[10]. Criminalizing the action of taking two seats

---

10 **65.000.000 (sixty five million)** Americans have a criminal record. (Alexander, 2010)

in the subway or allowing truancy by underage kids are examples of the bad use and selectivity of criminal laws[11].

However, there are scholars who advocate that these politics are the means for a terrifying ending, such as the opinion of Alexandra Natapoff (2014), analyzed before, regarding misdemeanors. Once the police force can hold and primarily detain an offender, the plea bargaining is installed, aiming to exclude from society, as long as possible, specific individuals – to be known: minorities.

As stated before, the prosecutions overcharging technique and discretionary in filling charges are tools to induce a guilty pleas. The criminalization of outskirt's conducts – such as littering, driving with an expired driving license, take up two sits in the subway, disorderly conduct and resisting arrest – when added up to a mass incarceration policy guaranteed by unconstitutional procedures, disrespecting the due process of law and the presumption of innocence can only lead to criminal selectivity with the massive incarceration of the poor people.

After analyzing the arguments existing against some aspects of the American plea bargaining system discussed, it is understood that they deserve close attention. Constitutional basic principles are being violated, as are basic human rights.

---

11 Many simple and common behaviors have been criminalized for the past decades. Standing on the sidewalk, drinking in public, jaywalking, loitering, littering, marijuana use, driving with an expired driving license, taking up two sits in the subway, disorderly conduct, resisting arrest, among others, are examples of misdemeanor conducts used by the criminal justice as a scope to impose fines, supervise and control part of America's society.

To respond to judicial tardiness is crucial to any democratic system, but to aim effectiveness undervaluing some of the most important principles of the democratic State based on the rule of the law cannot be the solution.

Reminding the words of George Fisher: "There is no glory in plea bargaining. In place of a noble clash for truth, plea bargaining gives us a skulking truce.[...] [It] may be, as some chronicles claim, the invading barbarian. But it has won all the same" (Fisher, 2003, p. 1).

— 4.4 —
Introduction to criminal procedure: trial process

If negotiation has not taken place during the pre-trial phase, the following stage is the trial process. Nonetheless, the plea bargaining procedure is available at any time, through any step of the way – including after hung jury's verdicts.

As we have discussed in the first chapter, jury's decisions must be unanimous, and a hung jury requires a new trial. At this point it is very common for the parties to negotiate a deal, due to the uncertainty surrounding the future final decision.

Coming back to the proceedings, if the case advances the first stages of the pre-trial process what we have next is the trial, post-trial motions, sentencing and appeal. A trial is scheduled after some weeks or months of the first appearance. In criminal cases, this part of the process is highly represented in movies and TV series – even though only 5% to criminal cases go to trial, all the rest are solved through the negotiating process.

There are two common trial proceedings, a bench trial and a jury trial. Bench trials happen before a single judge while a jury trial involves jurors. Bench trials are usually held in less serious offenses. For example, in the federal sphere, crimes in which there is a possibility the defendant is sentenced to jail, the accused has the right to be judged by a jury. In the state sphere, generally, offenses that may carry a sentence of less than six months in jail may be subjected to a bench trial.

The jury trial has been discussed before, and it starts with the Voir Dire stage (jury selection). When the trial takes place it starts with the parties opening statements, which consists in a summary of the case and the thesis each side is going to sustain and defend.

After the state has presented its case (the prosecution, that is the accusation party), a motion for direct verdict or a motion for acquittal may be filed – if that is the case. That may happen if the defense understands the evidence brought by the accusation is not sufficient to sustain a conviction.

If that is not the case or the court denies the motions, the next step regards the defense stating its case, bringing evidence and witnesses (expert or lay witnesses) to support its arguments in favor of the accused. It is important to remember that both parties have the right to cross-examine the witnesses testifying in court. Also, illegal evidence brought to court by the parties may be objected (such as illegally obtained ones and hearsay) (Wonsovicz, 2017).

Finally, it is time for closing arguments, summarizing and pointing the important evidence in favor of the defended thesis, also pointing out flaws and mistakes in the other party's arguments of evidence. Defense and prosecution state their cases to a jury that will deliberate, deciding if the accused is guilty, or not, of the charges pending against him. The jury's verdict must be unanimous or a new trial will be scheduled.

A judge does the criminal sentencing and that happens usually at the moment the accused pleads guilty (right after the plea bargaining negotiation) or after a jury has found him guilty. Sentences may vary according to their type. There are mandatory sentences, undetermined sentences, "three strikes" sentences, among others. If the sentencing does not happen immediately, as the magistrate needs time to decide about it, a sentence hearing will be held so the judge manifests the sentence applied to the case.

Then there is the phase of post-trial motions, usually filed to correct errors that may have occurred during trial. Some of the options are motions for a new trial, motions for judgment not withstanding verdict. A motion for a new trial is filed when there has been a legal error during trial and a motion for judgment not withstanding verdict, when the accused has been found guilty without the corroboration of sufficient evidence.

If these motions are denied, the defense may proceed to an appeal. The appeal is a proceeding, under which a higher court may review a lower court's decision. As we have seen, the common flow is the start of the proceedings in the district court, moving to the circuit courts as a second level of appeal and to the states' supreme court as a third level of appeal. The US Supreme court only analyses some of the cases filed, regarding constitutional issues.

However, a direct appeal may do some shortcuts. When a state's constitutional law is being questioned the intermediate level of appeal may be suppressed and the proceeding may be directed to the highest court within the jurisdiction. In California that also happens with Criminal cases to each a death penalty was imposed.

For those who are interested in comprehending the criminal trial dynamic there are some real case trials and proceedings that have become documentaries, TV series, available at video streaming platforms. Some really interesting ones are "The Staircase", "The Trials of Gabriel Fernandez" and "Making a Murderer".

"The Staircase" documentary tells the trial history of Michael Peterson, who was accused of murdering his own wife at their house. In the film, all the trial proceeding is very much explored in details and evidence rules can be analyzed, as the important part played by witnesses, especially expert witnesses. This case's images and trial proceedings are actually used at Evidence classes at University of California, to exemplify the evidence rules applied in court, which are discussed in class.

"The Trials of Gabriel Fernandez" is a more difficult documentary to watch, since it involves the violent murder of a 7-year-old child, Gabriel Fernandez, who had been submitted to long periods of torture, both physical and psychological, inflicted by his birth mother and her boyfriend. Also in here the trial has been carefully covered, and the proceedings' details are available to the viewer. In the case it is also discussed the efficiency of the system in protecting vulnerable children, once many social workers were also criminally accused and tried.

In this last documentary, "Making a Murderer", the TV series tells the story of Steven Avery, who was wrongly convicted of the crimes of sexual assault and attempted murder, spending 18 years in prison. The case involves coercion to obtain confession, inefficient legal defense, police corruption, and violation of the criminal defendant's constitutional rights, among others.

Once we have had an overview of the pre-trial and trial rules and proceedings, it is interesting to analyze the constitutional principles regarding the practices.

Legal Vocabulary Bank

- **Bench trial** – "A trial before a judge without a jury. * The judge decides questions of facts as well as questions of law." (Garner, 2016, p. 776)
- **Jury trial** – "A trial in which the factual issues are determined by a jury, not by the judge." (Garner, 2016, p. 776)
- **Hung jury** – "A jury that cannot reach a verdict by the required voting margin." (Garner, 2016, p. 424)
- **Death-qualified jury** – "A jury that is fit to decide a case involving the death penalty because the jurors have no absolute ideological bias against capital punishments." (Garner, 2016, p. 424)
- **Motion for judgment of acquittal** – "A criminal defendant's request, at the close of the government's case or the close of all evidence, to be acquitted because there is no legally sufficient evidentiary basis on which a reasonable jury could return a guilty verdict. * If the motion is granted the government has no right to appeal." (Garner, 2016, p. 497)
- **Motion for judgment notwithstanding the verdict** – "A party's request that the court enter a judgment in its favor despite the jury's contrary verdict because there is no legally sufficient evidentiary basis for a jury to find for the other party. [...]" (Garner, 2016, p. 497)

- **Motion for direct verdict** – "A party's request that the court enter judgment in its favor before submitting the case to the jury because there is no legally sufficient evidentiary basis for a jury to find for the other party." (Garner, 2016, p. 496)
- **Motion to strike** – "2. Evidence. A request that inadmissible evidence be deleted from the record and that the jury be instructed to disregard it." (Garner, 2016, p. 499). Differently, a motion to suppress is a request that inadmissible evidence never even get to court, as seen before.
- **Objection** – "A formal statement opposing something that has occurred, or is about to occur, in court and seeking the judge's immediate ruling on the point. * The party objecting must usu. State the basis for the objection to preserve the right to appeal an adverse ruling." (The Black Law's Dictionary, 2011, p. 527)

— 4.5 —

Constitutional Principles regarding criminal procedure

In the study of the legal English, it is interesting to have contact with the constitutional language and its peculiarities. For this reason we will observe the main constitutional principles regarding the criminal law and procedure.

American criminal statutes are guided by constitutional principles. As we have stated before, the constitutional rules are aimed to limit the scope of the state power, which encompasses the power to punish the people.

As we have seen before, the US Constitution has 7 articles and 27 Amendments. Most of the criminal law principles are brought by the Amendments. We are going to study them in order of appearance.

Just as an observation, the Constitution dispositions are usually divided in the legal provision (the article referred) and the text, from which a principle is extracted.

Article III, Section two, Clause Three, brings two main principles, which are the jury clause and the venue clause.

> **The Trial of all Crimes**, except in Cases of Impeachment, **shall be by Jury**; and such **Trial shall be held** in the State where the said Crimes shall have been committed; but when not committed within any State, the Trial shall be at such Place or Places as the Congress may by Law have directed. (The Constitution of the United States, 2021, Emphasis added)

According to the US Constitution the criminal defendant has the right to a jury trial that must happen where the crime has been committed. As we have seen, there exceptions to those principles and the accused can waive the jury trial right. The bench trial is an option in determined cases, for example. Also, as the own Constitution envisages, a jury trial may be moved to a different venue when that need is justified.

We have already discussed the 4th Amendment, since it brings the warrant requirement, seeking to protect peoples' individuality. The Constitution text is the one that follows:

> The right of the people to be secure in their persons, houses, papers, and effects, against unreasonable searches and seizures, shall not be violated, and no Warrants shall issue, **but upon probable cause, supported by Oath or affirmation,** and particularly describing the place to be searched, and the persons or things to be seized. (The Constitution of the United States, 2021)

Here we are facing the unreasonable searches and seizures clause, which is a very important clause, specially to the defense party, in order to avoid the use in court of illegally obtained evidence – that meaning, any searches or seizures conducted without a warrant, issued by a neutral judge. Also important to remember there are exceptions to the warrant requirement, which we have covered before. In those case the warrant can be waived.

The 5th Amendment is the source of many important principles. Its text stays that:

> No person shall be held to answer for a capital, or otherwise infamous crime, unless on a presentment or **indictment of a Grand Jury**, except in cases arising in the land or naval forces,

or in the Militia, when in actual service in time of War or public danger; nor shall any person be **subject for the same offence to be twice put in jeopardy** of life or limb; nor shall be compelled in any criminal case to be a **witness against himself**, nor be deprived of life, liberty, or property, without **due process of law**; nor shall private property be taken for public use, **without just compensation**. (The Constitution of the United States, 2021, Emphasis added).

Four principles are extracted from the Amendment, the grand jury, double jeopardy, self-incrimination and due-process clauses. As we have seen, the indictment, the formal and official written accusation, must be done by a grand jury proceeding if it relates to a serious crime.

A grand jury is formed by 16 to 23 people, who decide, after hearing the accusation, weather to issue the indictment against the accused. That decision is made once the jurors decide the evidence is strong enough to hold a suspect for trial. There must be present a reasonable belief that the suspect has committed the crime. The bill of indictment charges the suspect with a specific crime.

The double jeopardy clause, also present in the amendment, forbids a person to be prosecuted or sentenced twice for the same crime. The self-incrimination clause states that no one may be compelled to testify against themselves. Furthermore, the Miranda warning rule, as seen before, foresees that a suspect must be informed of this right as soon as he is detained or held by law enforcement officials. The arrestee has the right to also remain in silence.

The due process of law is a largely known principle in modern statutes, not only under the US jurisdiction. The clause aims the protection of private rights through rules and principles regarding legal proceedings, in order to avoid arbitrary and unfair deprivation of life, liberty or property.

It is a principle of the most importance regarding criminal defense, which supports the right to adversarial proceedings and the minimal requirements of notice and hearing when there is the risk of right's deprivation. The due process clause in the 5th Amendment is applied to the Federal Government and the states. The 14th Amendment only applies to the states.

The 6th Amendment provides multiple clauses, such as the speedy trial clause, public trial clause, impartial jury clause, vicinage clause, information clause, confrontation clause, compulsory process clause and assistance of counsel clause.

> In all criminal prosecutions, the accused shall enjoy the right to a **speedy and public trial**, by an **impartial jury** of the State and district **wherein the crime shall have been committed**, which district shall have been previously ascertained by law, and **to be informed** of the nature and cause of the accusation; to be **confronted with the witnesses** against him; to have **compulsory process** for obtaining witnesses in his favor, and to have the **Assistance of Counsel** for his defense. (The Constitution of the United States, 2021, Emphasis added)

The speedy trial clause relates to reasonable diligence. When deciding if that right has been violated the courts take in consideration the length of and the reason of the delay, also observing if there was prejudice to the accused. That trial must be public, that meaning, that anyone can observe.

We have discussed the impartial jury right during the Voir Dire and the challenges regarding the jurors' choice. Mostly, an impartial jury is composed by people who have no opinion about the case before its analyses and the trial development. They base their decision on the evidence presented only. People who are ideological or in any other way biased to the matter or the people being tried cannot be considered neutral to judge the facts.

The vicinage clause relates to the right the accused has to have his trial held in the place where the crime was committed. Also jurors must be selected by the accused's jurisdiction. The information clause refers to the right one has to be informed what the accusations against him are – what happens in a first appearance hearing and, formally, in the indictment procedure.

The confrontation clause arises from the due process one and relates to the accused's right to confront face-to-face the witnesses who testify against him and to cross-examine them. To cross-examination is the act of questioning opposing witnesses, with the purpose of discrediting her testimony.

The power of obtaining witnesses in the accused's favor is the substance of the compulsory process clause. That power is accomplished through the use of subpoenas, which is an order subjected to a penalty for failing to comply. Finally, the Amendment provides the counsel assistance clause, under which every criminal defendant has the right to be represented by a lawyer.

As we have seen, that principle can be relativized, once criminal offenses that are not penalized with jail time do not entitle the defendant to technical defense. Going further on the right to counseling, it is very discussed in the criminal system the issue regarding ineffective counseling. If a fair trial was denied to the accused because his defendant did an incomplete performance or did not give all the professional efforts to the case, a criminal conviction may be overturned – eve though the ineffective assistance is really hard to prove.

The ineffective assistance is proved through a two-prong test (Strickland v Washington, 466 U.S. 688 (1984)), where the defendant must show (1) that the counselor's performance fell below an "objective standard of reasonableness" and (2) "a reasonable probability that, but for counsel's unprofessional errors, the result of the proceeding would have been different".

There are largely known cases that can attest that reaching the test requisites is extremely hard. Technical assistances in which the defense lawyer slept during the witnesses' cross-examination, or whose defense attorney was senile or drunk during trial did not constitute inefficient assistance of counsel. (Kirchmeier, 1996, p. 455).

The 8th Amendment states says that: "Excessive bail shall not be required, nor excessive fines imposed, nor cruel and unusual punishments inflicted".

The clauses present in the Constitutional provision are the excessive bail and fine clause and the cruel and unusual punishment clause. For starters, a bail must be fixed in a reasonable amount, considering the risk the accused will not appear for trial and the seriousness of the crime. A judge imposes bail in the US, usually up to 48 hours after the accused has been arrested.

Research shows that a regular felony accused has its bail fixed in 55 thousand dollars, and to be released from custody the offender must pay 10% of the total amount. However, a felony offender general income is inferior to 7 thousand dollars a month, and, worst than that, almost 50% of the detained do not make enough money to post bail (Dobbie; Goldin; Yang, 2018, p. 1).

Despite the Constitutional excessive bail clause, the regular use of pre-trial detention, and the impossibility for the poor accused to post bail, have a great influence in the criminal convictions in the country. The reason for that are the facts that the high amount to be paid for freedom and the impossibility for posting bail may "can disrupt defendants' lives, putting jobs at risk and increasing the pressure to accept unfavorable plea bargains" (Dobbie; Goldin; Yang, 2018).

The private sector counts on bail bond dealers and agencies – many of which are also responsible for many activities within the private prison services. Through this professionals and companies it is possible to secure the bail amount that works as a bank loan.

One of the most well known American constitutional clauses is the other principle brought by the 8th Amendment: the prohibition of cruel and unusual punishment. When a person first reads the 8th Amendment rights, they automatically take her to the medieval times with its dungeons, and wooden wheels being used for punishment. In less than one second, this image of women accused of witchery being burned in huge fires, usually placed in the middle of public squares, under the population's applauses, appears in front of our eyes.

A lot of time has gone by and, as a society, we have evolved in many fields, especially in fields of knowledge, but the necessity of the 8th Amendment application has never been so latent, once the reality of punishment brutality is very alive among us.

For people who are not part of the judicial environment, or, in other way, do not engage in criminal justice practices, it might be a surprise the fact that cruel punishment is far away from being extinguished in modern society.

Physical punishment is a routine not only when thinking about the incarcerated, but also when analyzing the police activity on the streets and against the ones under investigation.

When it comes to the incarcerated, sexual abuse of inmates, physical injuries – also committed by penitentiary agents against the interns –, psychological abuse, overcrowding, disproportionality of the sentences, non observance of basic human rights – such as schooling, the right to work, to receive intimate visits and leisure – are some of the cruel and unusual forms of punishment being applied in our society.

We could go further and include among the above the lack of counsel assistance, supposed to be proportioned to the ones who face criminal charges. Even if some kind of counsel assistance may always be provided, we are not talking about a business law lawyer sitting to defend a murder accused. We are referring to the right of specialized counsel assistance, capable of truly defending the interests of the one placed in the dock.

In addition to that, there are the modern criminal politics to be critically analyzed. Policies such as "zero tolerance", "tree strikes and you are out" and the Actuarial Criminal Policy–with its absurd criteria – among others, are arbitrary, not to say worst, and can perfectly be considered as cruel and unusual punishment.

This principle was discussed in the case which opinion's we have analyzed and briefed in the previous chapter – Ewing v. California (538 U.S. 11 (2003)). In Ewing's case the issue regarding the 8th Amendment principle was weather the penalty of life in prison for stealing golf clubs, under the three strike's law, was not proportional, violating the prohibition of cruel and unusual punishment. The holding brought the understanding of the court that the Eight Amendment does not foresees the necessity of a criminal sentence being proportional. That meaning, disproportionate punishment would not be considered cruel or unusual – what was contested by the dissenting opinion.

Lastly, the death penalty comes as the cherry of the cake to this critical analysis. At this point it is not secure to affirm to be the capital punishment the queen of all cruel punishment forms, due to the reality of the prison system in our society. But, we can strongly affirm that it is one of the most bizarre ways of retribution of a crime to someone and that it is the literal translation of "unusual and cruel punishment".

Analyzing a clearer example of the problem, in the US the discussion regarding the cruelty of the death penalty is constant. The lethal injection effects on the human body before causing the death of the individual are polemic.

As a study in Ohio has discovered, the injection's fluid, that goes into the death sentenced, is composed by three substances, one of which is the Midazolam, that has been proved to cause pulmonary edema – what makes the convict to experience a drowning situation, having water accumulated in his lungs. "The autopsies showed the executed men felt the panic and terror of asphyxiation before they died" (Segura, 2019).

In addition to that there is space for discussion weather trying juveniles as adults, or life imprisonment penalties or even the sex offender registry for life are characterized as cruel or unusual punishments.

To end our analysis of constitutional provisions regarding criminal law and procedure principles, the fourteenth Amendment discusses the states' due process clause and the equal protection clause.

All persons born or naturalized in the United States, and subject to the jurisdiction thereof, are citizens of the United States and of the State wherein they reside. No State shall make or enforce any law which shall abridge the privileges or immunities of citizens of the United States; **nor shall any State deprive any person of life, liberty, or property, without due process of law; nor deny to any person within its jurisdiction the equal protection of the laws.** (Library of Congress, 2021, Emphasis added)[12]

The equal protection clause guarantees that the government must treat persons from all classes equally under the law. The rational behind the clause is class and race equality under similar circumstances. It is aimed to avoid discrimination and if that discrimination is present in a statute, it has to be rationalized, as explained by Garner (2011, p. 271):

> In today's jurisprudence, equal protection means that legislation that discriminates must have a rational basis for doing so. And if the legislation affects a fundamental right (such as the right to vote) or involves a suspect classification (such as race), it is unconstitutional unless it can withstand strict scrutiny.

Analyzing constitutional principles brings an understanding on the rational behind the criminal laws and the practices in the

---

12   United States Constitution. Available at: <https://www.senate.gov/civics/resources/pdf/US_Constitution-Senate_Publication_103-21.pdf>.

US justice system. It is also really important getting familiar with the language, since it is commonly used in court, in the daily practice or in law academic programs, thus, very important for the ones who practice the law or study abroad.

— 4.6 —
Prison policies

Since the end of the 20th century a new economic-criminal regime is installed in the US, which envisages the promotion of a more severe penal policy, seeking to decrease the country's criminality rates – what has culminated in a prison population growth, which is four times bigger.

The welfare state has suffered rigorous changes, having been adopted the workfare state, what started a crusade against social benefit policies. The rational was that the excess of public assistance to the poor people would be the responsible factor regarding poverty high rates, due to its incentives to inactivity – what would end up reflected in the urban violence.

A way of combating the unemployment situation, restoring economy, would be ceasing the public aid, or drastically reducing it, in addition to the union's dismantling, the relativisation of labor rules and the instauration of compulsory work requirement – workfare policies – for those who depend on state's assistance. The secret to success would be less state interference in the economy policies, based on the work of Charles Murray, and his book *Losing Ground* – a study that has never been empirically proved, by the way and that very criticized in its findings (Wacquant, 2011).

This new rational took in consideration the fact that, regarding public safety policies and the criminality rates decrease, the government does not need to question the reason for people to commit crimes. The state's part and obligation resumes to punish those who disobey the law. Opposing to the rational regarding economy, when it comes to criminal policies, the state becomes a giant, the bigger its interference, the better.

According to Murray, a judicial system exists to punish the guilty offenders, compensate the innocent, defending the interests of those citizens who respect the law (Wacquant, 2011). Based on Murray and Manhattan Institute's unproved theories, such as the one known as "The Broken Windows[13]", the law enforcement work was completely rearranged in the country, acting under a criminological basis, coordinated by William Bratton, who would become the New York's mayor, Rudolph Giuliane, main person in applying the zero tolerance policy.

Thus, aiming the public safe sensation of New York's upper classes, the zero tolerance policy starts a permanent persecution of the poor people and minorities in public areas, with an increase – of ten times – in the numbers of police officers,

---

13 This theory states that targeting minor crimes repression by the police would crate a lawful environment, preventing serious crimes from happening, since, for the theory's supporters, anti-social behavior and civil disorder would encourage the crime commitment.

resulting in instantaneous intervention of the law force and the inflexible application of the law for misdemeanor conducts – such as drunkenness, begging, threats, among other behaviors which can be considered antisocial, usually attached to the lower class citizens.

The new approach regarding crime repression resulted in many violent episodes regarding police activities, with unjustified homicides, rapes, and aggressive practices in general by the zero tolerance riot police – 380 police officers, almost all of them being white, who were also suspects of proceeding detentions due to racial profiling, systemically mocking the accused's constitutional rights (Wacquant, 2011).

Pursuant to the National Urban League, this police party, in two years, has stopped and searched 45 thousand people under mere suspicion, based on these person's clothing, appearance, behavior and – above any indication – due to their skin color. 82% of these detentions had been revealed unnecessary and the accusations on the 18% left were considered null or have been invalidated by courts in half of the cases. Only 4 thousand detentions out of 45 thousand, were justified, 1 in 11 (Wacquant, 2011, p. 43).

Giuliani's tactics start to be seriously questioned and statistics show that 80% of young black and Latin man in New York have been detained and searched at least one by the police.[14] However, there are opposing understandings regarding the police activity

---

14 "Those NYPD blues", US News & World Report, April 5th, 1999, in Wacquant, 2011, p. 43.

in New York, once most black people consider the police force a danger, not making them feel safer and, on the contrary, 87% of the white people praise the new policy, feeling safer.[15]

The police brutality in the US is still an actual discussion, specially regarding the violence against black people. In 2013 a movement has been started in the country under the name "Black People Matter". Its campaign encompasses the repulse to violence and racism towards African-Americans. The protests relate to black people killings by police officers, racial profiling, the police brutality and judicial inequality in the criminal justice system regarding black people (blacklivesmatter.com).

To bring a recent example of police brutality against the black community, on May 2020 George Floyd was chocked to death by a police officer, who was being filmed, in Minnesota. The recording shows George groaning and saying to the officer, repeatedly, that he could not breath. George worked as a security guard in a restaurant and the case has spread world widely[16].

This contextualization of the American public safety policies is important to understand the prison population in the US According to the Bureau of Statistics (2019) the prison population in the country is composed by 2.200.000 people, currently accommodated in federal and states' prisons and jails. Most of

---

15 "Poll in New York finds many think police are biased", *The New York Times*, 16 mar 1999, in Wacquant, 2011, p. 45.

16 Available at: <www.bbc.com/news/world-us-canada-52806572>. Acess on April 6th, 2021.

the incarcerated are in state institutions. That numbers shows that for every 100 thousand Americans, 665 are imprisoned.

The prison population could represent the 10th biggest city in the country, only behind grand population centers such as New York, Los Angles and Chicago. According to official data from the justice department, the prison system costs to the government up to 80 billion dollars a year, while the public money invested in the education sector amounts 65 billion dollars a year.

Racial minorities, such as African-Americans and Latin people, in great part, compose the incarcerated population. It is interesting to understand that black people represent 12% of the American general population, however, in prison, they represent one third of the incarcerated.

As to the crimes committed by the ones who are in prison, a FBI report (2018) points out that more than 10 million Americans were arrested in 2018, and regarding their crimes, 1.654.282 people committed drug related crimes (among these, 86% were arrested not due to drug commercialization but drug possession).

Arrests relating to crimes against property added up 1.167.296. There were also 25.205 arrests due to rape crimes and 11.970 arrests due to homicides. DUIS were responsible for more than 1.000.000 Americans going to prison in that year. In America people go to jail a lot, and that happens for many reasons.

Researches state that putting an end to the war on drugs would not be enough to control the mass incarceration phenomenon. Four out of five people are in jail for crimes not related to drugs, which are more or less serious offenses. To achieve a prison population decrease it would be necessary to review how the justice system responds to crime commitment, from the most serious offenses – with the imposition of life sentences, to petty crimes, which encompass flash detentions yet, exert a huge burden on the offender due to their conviction's collateral consequences (Sawer; Wagner, 2020).

With more than 2 million people behind bars, prison conditions and policies are questioned in that system. Reports bring complaints regarding the practice of torture, sexual abuse, homicides, official guard's corruption in overcrowded institutions (Equal Justice Initiative, 2019).

The justice department's data attest that Alabama jails are the most violent ones, where the inmate's constitutional rights are routinely violated. It is reported sexual abuse and murder among inmates, a facilitated drug commercialization environment, and the practice of extortion, threats and torture with the guard's connivance.

Moreover, it is denounced the increase of the number of people with mental diseases in jails, who have severe limited access to treatment, leading to many cases of suicide. Besides the lack of technical experience in identifying potential suicidal by prison workers and the absence of adequate treatment, one can see a high use of solitary confinement in those institutions (Equal Justice Initiative, 2019).

The legislator's primordial idea when instituting the solitary confinement was to separate and isolate the leaders of criminal organizations from other prisoners as much as punishing inmates for their misbehavior within the prison walls. The solitary confinement might have been the tool found to deal with prison violence resulting from the process of mass incarceration-phenomenon emerged in the 80's – with the overcrowding of prison population. But it has not been restricted to that.

With ideologies of "tough on crime", "war on drugs" and the [almost delusional] search for public safety, solitary confinement has also being used to extract information of supposed gang members about the criminal organization they might be affiliated to, as one of the few ways to be released from isolation is by debriefing (Ruiz v. Brown, Case No. C 09-05796 CW, 2012).

With these objectives, the solitary confinement gained popularity based on the fact that it would increase safety in penal establishments, being in the Government's hands the internal control of prisons – a control that was threatened by internal violence and corruption by the inmates. Despite that, many question are being raised regarding the regime's constitutionality.

The solitary confinement determination is viewed by many as an inhumane apartheid of the inmate, or a method of personality annihilation, what violates the human dignity as much as the physical integrity of the prisoner (what can be easily identified in Ruiz v. Brown and in the Testimony of Professor Craig Haney (2012), where the physiological and physical side effects of the inmates isolation are being described).

Many also make severe critics to the length of isolation, that in some cases has reached more than 20 years, as much as the fact that not only dangerous felons are being subjected to the regime, but also people who carry a list of misdemeanors in their pockets.

Not advancing in the critics regarding the psychological effects of the isolation, a large share of criminal specialists understand that the confinement isolation violates the 8th and 14th amendments, once inmates subjected to the practice of are deprived of the minimal measure of life's necessities and are being violated in their dignity and their right to be free from cruel and unusual punishment. On the other hand, the court's understanding of deprivation of basic human rights and the liability of the officer's of the system differ from the common criminological sense, as expressed in Wilson v. Saiter (501 US 294, 1991) and in Farmer v. Brennan (501 US 825, 1994).

In Wilson, the conditions of imprisonment can only violate the Eighth Amendment if the culpable state of mind of the agents can be proved (even if the alleged violation is continued and systemic). It is also stated by the court that specific deprivation of human basic rights needs to be proved–such as hunger for example. In Farmer, deliberated indifference is required in order to prove an Eighth Amendment violation, thus, the officer's liability. It must be proved the officers knew about substantial risk of serious harm and failed to take reasonable measures to abate it.

Despite the controversy stated, and in connection with Constitutional violations, in all the cases being analyzed one major violation of modern society laws is being presented before us, that being the violation of the "Rule of Law". One of its principles is that "the laws are clear, publicized, stable, and just; are applied evenly; and protect fundamental rights, including the security of persons and property" (Justice Speaker International, 2021).

Specifically regarded to the exigency for the laws to be clear, publicized, stable and just, the isolation confinement – and its release – is surrounded by discretionary, since there is no time limit being applied to the inmates in isolations, with some of them being submitted to the practice for 10 to 20 years (even though the original idea of the program was not for it to last more than 21 months) (Ruiz v. Brown).

A further complicating factor is that the inmate subjected to isolation is not aware of the requisites for his release, what makes difficult to precise which exact conducts might lead to one's exclusion of solitary confinement.

> the policy of retaining prisoners in the SHU who are not active gang affiliates, or against whom no reliable evidence exists that they present any threat of gang-related violence or misconduct, is unmoored from any legitimate penological purpose or security need. [...] That leads them to reasonably believe that there is no way out of the SHU except to debrief or die. (Casella; Hidgeway, 2011)

It is very easy to identify the practices and laws evolving solitary confinement as not clear nor stable and just. Furthermore, once isolation is used against inmates who do not present any threat of gang-related violence or misconduct they are also not being used to secure prison safety, which is its main justification.

Finally, recidivism is a topic of major critics when it comes to isolation of inmates. As a result of isolation (which encompasses very few to the inexistence of social contact), "many prisoners are significantly handicapped when they attempt to make their eventual transition from prison back into the free world. [...] Indeed, there are some recent, systematic evidence that time spent in solitary confinement contributes to elevated rates of recidivism" (Haney, 2012, p. 3).

Additionally, reports from the justice department state that half of the states' jails inmates respond to the criteria regarding chemical dependency, besides the fact that many of them suffer from serious types of mental diseases – almost a third of the incarcerated women. Little or no treatment is designated to these population (Bureau of Statistics, 2017).

Death rates inside prisons have increased 500% in the last years, figuring among the causes of inmate deaths homicides, accidents, alcohol use related events and untreated medical problems. As we are going to see ahead, private companies offer most of medical treatment services in prisons. Therefore, the US prison system also registries serious problems, even under the private administration of these establishments.

One hundred and twenty one (121) correctional institutions in the country are run by private companies – that means, 9% of all facilities. Nonetheless, the country has the larger private prison population in the globe, which generates profits around 4 billion dollars a year.

Private prisons have been proved to be less safe, not promoting the inmate rehabilitation, also being expensive to the public safes. The private practice also increases the number of the incarcerated under their administration (Equal Justice Initiative, 2019). Those are some of the reasons why 22 American states have banished the prison privatization policy. Among the states that adept the policy the incarceration rates in the private sector has been rising, totalizing a 77% growth since 2000 (Sentencing Project, 2019).

The private companies celebrate long-term contracts with the public administration, fixating a fee per inmate that the state must cover, guaranteeing a minimal number of prisoner in each contract, working as a criticized perverse incentive for sending people to jail (Sentencing Project, 2019). Another critic is that prison conditions on private facilities are not better than the one found in the public ones.

Besides the contracts referred before, private companies are also responsible for providing some types of services to the prison population, such as phone and video calls, food, laundry, electronic monitoring devices, for what a fee is charged. Health and medical care are also provided by private companies in many prisons, even though in an insufficient or, in some cases, inexistent way. Reports indicate the contractors' denial to medical treatment to inmates or the treatment of serious medical situations with ibuprophen, contributing to the high rates of death in prison (Sainato, 2019).

Private facilities are also less safe than public ones, once they present more cases of threat to inmates' physical safety. Also, in those facilities illegal activities are favored, such as illegal product commercialization, attacks, riots, with a higher necessity of the use of force and more cases regarding prison officers' abuse.

These situations may be justified by the fact that private companies aim to profit from their services, therefore, they tend to cut expenses relating to prison safety, rehabilitation programs and health care, fore example.

Finally, the quest for maximum profit leads to the incarceration of the biggest number of people, for the longest time possible, what has an impact on policies regarding over criminalization of conducts, longer imprisonment periods and obstructed parole and probation benefits.

Regardless of the nature of the prison or jail administration, privately or publicly run, the prison costs can, and usually, be charged of the prisoner once he is released, under the risk of being sent back to jail if he fails to do so. The pay-to-stay laws and the debtor's prisoners are another issues of the American prison system.

The understanding involving both court's and prison's "care and maintenance" costs changed a lot since they were first discussed by the Supreme Court – in Williams v. Illinois (1970). During the 70's, the court was used to hold the opinion that the individual's failure to pay fines and court's costs should not allow the criminal system to send him back to jail, under penalty of violating the Equal Protection Clause. In Tate v. Short (401 U.S. 395, 1971), the understanding was that, in such case, imprisonment was imposed solely to augment the state's revenues, with no penal objective, even though no revenue could be augment by imprisoning Tate, an indigent, who would have to be feed and taken car of by the state.

This understanding was developed and relativized in following cases. It had been changed from the "no right to imprisonment at all" – passing by a gray area of impositions of conditions to the imprisonment (such as the proof that the individual was responsible for the failure to pay fines and court's costs and the existence of adequate alternative forms of punishment) (Bearden v. Georgia, 461 US 660 (1983)) – in the actual conjuncture, to the "complete and total right to imprison" the individual for failing to pay his debts with the criminal justice (included here the costs while incarcerated), as much as conceiving the state the power to attach prisoner's income of any type – including social security benefits – even on a pre-trial stage, based solely on probable cause (Ham v. South Carolina, 409 US 524 (1973)).

The change was significantly impacted by the economic crisis experienced by America in recent years and the "incarceration boom" (and consequent criminal system's cost increase), and it was based on the rationales of deterrence, rehabilitation, retribution and its popularity among tax payers (Andolena, 2010, p. 99).

The question to be made in face of the present scenario is if the understanding held in the first cases during the 70's (the violation of equal protection cause and the impossibility of augment the state's revenues) have also changed over the years.

By analyzing the shift on the Court's opinion about imprisoning individuals for failing to pay court' costs and their maintenance fee from while imprisoned, it becomes clear that the state could not support this burden anymore. Thus, due to the "incarceration boom" experienced by America since the 80's, due to the economic crisis faced most recently by the US, and the fact that the total corrections expenditures rank as the fifth largest area of state spending, an alternative to the system should be presented, and the "pay-to-stay" program could have been a progress in that aspect.

Furthermore, it could be argued that billing individuals and their families for the costs they represent to the system is not only fair (since inside walls they are feed, dressed and assisted), but may also serve as both deterrence and rehabilitation tools, inhibiting crime commitment.

In the worst-case scenario, the billing system would bring a social appraisement and it has proved to be "popular among tax payers" (Andolena, 2010, p. 90). during the resection period, when "good citizens" struggle to feed and assist their families. There is also the mass understanding that "inmates should be made to pay for their crimes – literally" (Andolena, 2010, p. 90).

The counterarguments for the shift in the court's understanding of the subject are many. Starting with the ideas of deterrence and rehabilitation, it could be argued that once an inmate is released with a significant amount of debt it is really likely of him to reencounter the criminal activity as a way of relieving himself of the burden. (Andolena, 2010, p. 109). Neither deterrence nor rehabilitation may be applied to these cases. Furthermore, by placing the burden on inmate's friends and family the personal responsibility of the accused for the crime committed stops existing, being this responsibility unlawfully extended and "placing the burden on the wrong people" (Andolena, 2010, p. 109). The lack of penal objectives in billing the inmate supported by the court on the 70's can be affirmed.

The main ideal that sending released citizens back to prison, for failing to accomplish financial burdens derived from their passage through the criminal system, would violate The Equal Protection Clause may be still defendable. In the state of California 88% of jail inmates were unemployed or earned less than $1000 per month by the time of the arrest. It is more than probable that this great majority of inmates will not be able to bear the costs of their passage through the criminal system, while only a small percentage might do so. "Serious fairness and equality concerns are raised" since wealthier accused are safer when it comes to be put back into prison (Andolena, 2010, p. 121).

Another argument that could be made related to the inequality raised by the "pay-to-stay" law is the existence of safer, cleaner and more secure facilities for inmates who are able to pay its fee, that varies from $75 to $175 per night, to serve their sentences, staying away from "the chaotic county jails" (Andolena, 2010, p. 120). Since 88% of jail inmates in California were unemployed or earned less than $1000 per month by the time of the arrest, it becomes clear the inequality rose by the program.

Finally, it could be argued that the main objective of the Court's understanding shift, to ease the burden on the state to financially support a criminal system, which covers in total more than 5 million citizens, has failed. The great majority subjected to the criminal system is poor and the "pay-to-stay programs rarely are profitable". It has been found that the system is "spending more money in their efforts to collect the fees than they are able to collect" (Andolena, 2010, p. 120).

Based on all the counterarguments made, one conclusion may be that the only plausible reason to keep the program going, regardless the Court's understanding at the 70's (the violation of the Equal Protection Clause, the lack of penal objectives and the impossibility to augment state's revenue) is that the program is popular with the public (Andolena, 2010, p. 107).

Regarding American prison policies another topic that is really interesting to understand relates to the alternatives to incarceration, more specific probation programs.

Probation was created as an option to reduce the use of jail sentences for first-time offenders (Taxman, 2102, p. 365). It started as good policy, to give non-violent crimes a punishment alternative, different from incarceration.

As the "War on Drugs" and the America's search for a more efficient police when it comes to punishing – orchestrated by the neoliberal agenda – lead to the generalized implementation of administrative punishment practices. Abandoning the ideals of scientific studies related to crime determinations and the processes of criminalization, all that became to matter were statistics related to the criminality risk's factors.

The updated numbers are alarming, since the probation population is almost twice the number of people in jail (Andolena, 2010, p. 363), what shows that America has embraced the shortcut, preferring the less bureaucratic way of charging and punishing its population. Probation is also being used as a supplementary punishment – to be served after incarceration or simply as a way of supervising the released ones (Andolena, 2010, p. 368).

Probation agencies offer treatment services to the probationers, what could be argued has a lot of practical impacts on the probationer's reinsertion into society. But it can also easily be argued that these services (such as mental health counseling, substance abuse assessment, life skills management, among others) are not only frequently unavailable, but also do not cover the main tool to develop a person into a citizen, which is education.

Probationers, in general, do not hold a high school degree and almost 65% of them are young adults, no older than 34 (Andolena, 2010, p. 368). If the main objective of parole's policies are to closely watch the probationer, monitoring his behavior, his social and work relations, giving a chance for him to fit in society and to change his values, learning how to abandon crime habits, the only way one might actually achieve that is trough the individual's capacitation to be in the work market[17], and that is only possible trough educational development.

It could be argued that job's positions are available in a daily basis, and that with a "little" effort everyone can change their own reality. This capitalist speech may have some impact on the middle class society, where the tools to pursue success are almost always available. When it comes to the preferable clients of the criminal system thing are different, those being "black male high school drop-outs" (Phelps, 2014, p. 2).

First of all, the individuals subjected to the criminal system usually live by the outskirts of the town, not really well served by public transportation and not close to the commonly available job positions. Secondly, without a school degree, the positions they have access to turn to be underpaid, with a low possibility

---

17 "Nearly 1 in 5 persons in federal prison committed his or her crime to obtain money for drugs" (Federal Sentencing Reporter, Vol. 22, No I, page 50, IV- A).

of promotion in a short term – what makes it hard to compete with the options available in the underworld of drug/guns trafficking, and other illegal activities.

In third place comes the fact that we are inserted in a society that is moved by mass consumption. We are subjected to the culture of "having before being", and this same society imposes goals, or high success conquests for its members, not necessarily giving them the means to achieve that – at list not democratically speaking. Many individuals end up finding their own way of achieving the goals they are expected to, in order to be successful – that meaning being able to consume – and unfortunately for most of them that implicates in engaging in illegal activities.

Furthermore, social behavior and life values are deeply connected to the environment one is inserted – as much as to his friends and family. If the community a person lives in does not offer the basic support to the human development (as housing conditions, health assistance, schooling, public transportation, among others) hardly ever ones efforts to change his behavior and life values will be achieve successfully.

It is really not a surprise that many probationer's fail to meet the program's requirements and end up in jail. But, it can be said that the policy can be considered successful, since 73% of its adepts complete the supervision (Taxman, 2011, p. 371). And here, again, we can see the state acting unfairly to the minorities. As opposed to the incarceration statistics, most probationers are

Caucasian and – based on the stated above and the existing research that "more privileged defendants are more likely to be sentenced probation rather than imprisonment" (Phelps, 2014, p. 16) – it can be argued they find it easier to accomplish the probation requirements (fine payment, drug testing, monthly meetings, among others).

As it occurs with mass imprisonment, mass probation can also be considered a new form of racialized domination (Phelps, 2014, p. 6). Domination over the poor people and the unfitted, with their constant surveillance and the imposition of goals almost impossible of achievement, "including conditions prohibiting behavior that is not criminal" (Doherty, 2013, p. 960).

For the most pessimists, or realistic, the system's objective is creating a legion of dummies or robots, which are systematically controlled and which act as they are expected to, not living much space for free and regardless actions, based on emotions and common mistakes. The state is prohibiting certain people to experience life and act as humans.

It could be argued society is demanding absurdly more exactly from the ones who can deliver absurdly less. "They" are expected to behave strictly according to moral and law rules, "they" should be able to overcome any difficulty, "they" should work harder to achieve success, "they" should manage the lack of education and the most basic rights – such as housing and health care – "they" should conform to the fact that "they" can not be like the "rest of us".

The criminal justice main clients live in a constant situation of violence. They have their rights and dignity violated, also experiencing physical and psychological violence. That being said, if US soldiers, who have being fighting in Iraq, have the benefits of parole for having a traumatic violence experience for a year or more (PBSNews, Veterans Suspected of Crimes Swap Guilty Pleas for Rehabilitation), this population – the criminal justice main clients – should have all kinds of criminal justice benefits, just for that fact of surviving to the most extreme circumstances and living under this generalized state of violence. They are constantly at war – not for a year or two, but for life, since they were born.

Finally, the US criminal justice is also know regarding its post-conviction effects, as we have stated before with sex offenders registry. However, not only that extreme crime leaves tracks on the life of an ex-offender. All people who go through the system are entitled with a criminal record, which has great impact in an individual's free life in society.

Criminal Records may be considered as new "birth certificates", given to those who have been convicted of a crime or misdemeanor, but they are not limited to that. Are also entitled to this document people who were arrested but never convicted of any crime – as in the case of Jose Gabriel Hernandes' mistaken identity, when he was wrongfully arrested for sexual assault (The Wall Street Journal, 2014). The wrongfully convicted are also awarded with the record, and to delete or expunge it may be a very difficult thing to do, as the study of 118 exonerated inmates found that one third still had a criminal record (The New York Times, 2013).

In the US, a criminal record is a permanent and public document. Sixty five million people have criminal records, which work as a prison label and a perpetual sanction also called as "internal exile" (Alexander, 2010, p. 142). With this new birth certificate in hands, many civil rights are diminished or annulled (as the right to vote, for example), and it makes the record's holder reentry in society very difficult, once the "growing obsession with background checking and commercial exploitation of arrest and conviction records makes it all but impossible for someone with a criminal record to leave the past behind" (The Wall Street Journal, 2014).

It could be argued that the American practice of complete access to the criminal history information is justified, especially because of "the belief people have a legitimate interest in being informed about the character of persons" with whom their life is shared, reinforcing the idea of "just deserves" and deterrence, sought by the record's policy (Jacobs; Larrauri, 2013, p. 15). As argued before, using the above rationale, citizens have the society's permission to hate the "criminal's social group". "They are entitled to no respect and little moral concern. [...] criminals today are deemed a characterless and purposeless people, deserving of our collective scorn and contempt" (Alexander, 2010, p. 141).

By contrast, advocates militate against the broad access to criminal records, their commercial exploitation and grossly trivialization. These practices happen in violation to the presumption of innocence principle, ignoring the social stigma created to the offender and resulting in the inability to social reintegration. They also hurt the right to privacy.

Other major concern is about the errors regularly found in criminal records and the existing barriers to correct them or delete criminal records in general. Anyone who is arrested, even if never convicted at trial, anyone who is wrongfully convicted and anyone who has complied the judgment, and is free to reenter society, has a criminal record. Based on the justifications for the publicity of these records already stated above, in some states, the centralized court administration agency sells criminal record information to private vendors (Jacobs; Larrauri, 2013). Anyone can buy these databases as forms of background check, and a lot of its information is available at Google.

The situation is more preoccupying when we acknowledge that most of the criminal records contain errors in them. A study in New York found that 87% of DCJS rap sheets contained some kind of error. On the FBI sphere 45% of the arrest files dispositions and on the private database world show "significant problems, including criminal identity theft leading to improperly attributed convictions, false positives and mismatches on non-biometric background check; and negligence by commercial vendors (The Consequences of Criminal Proceedings in New York State, 2015,

p. 6). In order to get the mistake corrected or the wrong record deleted, these private companies charge fees (The Wall Street Journal, 2014). Another problem faced by the record holders are the courts database failure storage management. Precious Daniels case is a proof of that- she had a criminal record for disorderly conduct and needed to "clean" her name for a job position, but the court "didn't have a record" (The Wall Street Journal, 2014).

The correctional facilities' crisis is not restricted to poor countries where incarceration is adopted. As one can see, well-developed and rich countries, like the US, share many of the underdeveloped nations' problems regarding public safety policies and the prison system. It is our duty, as academics of law, do debate the current policies in the law systems we are inserted, many of which are deeply inspired by the ones existing in North America.

Conclusion

This book had as its purpose to guide international students through the comprehension of the Legal English language. But we actually wanted to go further, helping students to comprehend the law rationalization in the American law system context, both in the academic environment and in the daily practice.

In order to achieve that, the legal education methods were studied, with emphasis to the case method, once the common law practice is based on precedent's analysis and ruling application.

We took time to understand how case briefing is done, what is the main information that needs to be extracted from a judicial opinion. For that, we also dedicated to analyze the opinion's structures, with the judicial reasoning, paying attention to argumentative strategies, made in a dialectic structure, calling attention to the importance of addressing counterarguments main theses.

We have worked with legal vocabulary and principles through-out the book, calling attention to their meaning whenever necessary, always contextualizing them in the text. And we believe to have covered great part of them. We have also discussed important legal practice vocabulary, such as the documents and persons in court and court language, highlighting the necessary verbs that are regularly applied in this environment.

In order to facilitate the understanding of all this information and connecting the dots as how to use it in a practical manner, we have framed it to real case scenarios, with case analysis, also taking some time to comprehend the justice system in the United States.

That is what most Legal English books and courses cover as their content. We took a further step; bringing to discussion, in an introductory way, some criminal laws and procedure statutes. And the intention here was to initiate the reader in the American criminal justice system, aiming international students who are not familiar with the statutes, policies and particularities of that system, which are many.

Moreover, we have summarized the main constitutional principles regarding the criminal laws and practice, elucidating their application and discussion along the text in judicial opinions.

We have also tried to demonstrate their importance in other policies discussions regarding prison policies and practices. All the debates that were brought are actual and not restricted to the American justice culture, being present in law systems around the globe.

Our objective here was to elucidate the legal vocabulary, discussing a little of the English grammar, focusing in the legal writing. But it was also our intention to introduce the legal practice in the U.S. legal system, preparing the international student to the law school environment and discussions, that he will eventually face, especially in the criminal area of knowledge, but not restricted to that, since the rationales discussed are extended to all areas that encompass litigation.

The idea was to approach the Legal English study in an innovative and deeper manner, not being restricted to the comprehension of not contextualized language and vocabulary. We think to have achieved that.

References

ACLU. **New Model Shows Reducing Jail Population will Lower COVID-19 Death Toll for All of Us**. URL: <https://www.aclu.org/news/smart-justice/new-model-shows-reducing-jail-population-will-lower-covid-19-death-toll-for-all-of-us/>. Accessed: 7 Apr. 2021.

ALEXANDER, M. **The New Jim Crow**: Mass Incarceration in the Age of Colorblindness. New York: The New Press, 2010.

ALSCHULER, A. W. The Prosecutor's Role in Plea Bargaining. **The University of Chicago Law Review**, v. 36, ano 1, Article 3. URL: <https://chicagounbound.uchicago.edu/uclrev/vol36/iss1/3>. Accessed: 1º Apr. 2021.

BERGMAN, P.; GOODMAN, P. D.; HOLM, T. W. **Cracking the Case Method**: Legal Analysis for Law School Success. Vandeplas: Heathrow, EUA: 2012.

BISHARAT, G. E. The Plea Bargain Machine. **Dilemas**: Revista de Estudos de Conflito e Controle Social, v. 7, n. 3, p. 767-795, July/Aug./Sep. 2014. URL: <https://revistas.ufrj.br/index.php/dilemas/article/download/7242/5824>. Accessed: 1º Apr. 2021.

BORDENKIRCHER V. HAYES. URL: <https://supreme.justia.com/cases/federal/us/434/357/>. Accessed: 7 Apr. 2021.

BRADY V. MARYLAND. URL: <https://supreme.justia.com/cases/federal/us/373/83/>. Accessed: 7 Apr. 2021.

BUREAUS OF JUSTICE STATISTCS. URL: <https://www.bjs.gov/content/pub/pdf/cpus16.pdf>. Accessed: 1º Apr. 2021.

BUREAUS OF JUSTICE STATISTCS. **Drug Use, Dependence, and Abuse Among State Prisoners and Jail Inmates, 2007-2009**. 2017. URL: <https://www.bjs.gov/content/pub/pdf/dudaspji0709.pdf>. Accessed: 1º Apr. 2021.

CALIFORNA COURTS. URL: <https://www.courts.ca.gov/2129.htm>. Accessed: 1º Apr. 2021.

CALIFORNIA LEGISLATIVE INFORMATION. URL: <https://leginfo.legislature.ca.gov/faces/codesTOCSelected.xhtml?tocCode=PEN>. Accessed: 7 Apr. 2021a.

CALIFORNIA LEGISLATIVE INFORMATION. Code Section Group. URL: <https://leginfo.legislature.ca.gov/faces/codes_displayText.xhtml?lawCode=PEN&division=&title=1.&part=1.&chapter=&article=>. Accessed: 7 Apr. 2021.

CARROLL V. UNITED STATES. URL: <https://supreme.justia.com/cases/federal/us/267/132/>. Accessed: 7 Apr. 2021.

CASELLA, J. HIDGEWAY, J. **Who are the hunger strikes**? How prisoners end at Pelican's Bay SHU? 2011. Solitary Watch. URL: <https://solitarywatch.org/2011/07/18/who-are-the-hunger-strikers-how-prisoners-land-in-pelican-bays-shus/>. Accessed: 7 Apr. 2021.

CHEMERINSKY, E.; LEVENSON, L. L. **Criminal Procedure**: Investigation. 3. ed. New York: Aspen, 2018. (Aspen Casebook Series).

COCHRANE, as Liqdr. URL: <https://casetext.com/case/cochrane-as-liqdr-v-f-e-c-ry-co>. Accessed: 1º Apr. 2021.

COLGAN, B. Constitutional Criminal Procedure Lectures at University of California – UCLA. Law 202, Fall Semester, 2014.

DEPARTMENT OF COMMERCE AND LABOR. Bulletin of the Bureau of Labor. Washington: Washington Government Printing Office, 1911.

DAVID, R. **Os grandes sistemas de direito contemporâneo**. 5. ed. São Paulo: Martins Fontes, 2014.

DIETER, M. S. **Política criminal atuarial**: a criminologia do fim da história. Rio de Janeiro: Renavan, 2013.

DOBBIE, W.; GOLDIN, J.; YANG, C. S. The Effects of Pretrial Detention on Conviction, Future Crime, and Employment: Evidence from Randomly Assigned Judges. **American Economic Review**, n. 108, ano 2, p. 201-240, 2018. URL: <https://pubs.aeaweb.org/doi/pdf/10.1257/aer.20161503>. Accessed: 1º Apr. 2021.

DOHERTY, F. Indeterminate Sentencing Returns: The Invention of Supervised Release. **New York University Law Review**, v. 88, 2013.

DOLOVICH, S. **Criminal Law Seminar at University of California – UCLA**. Spring Semester, 2014.

DOLOVICH, S. **Post Conviction Law and Policies**. University of California – UCLA, Spring semester 2014. Topics in Post-Conviction Law & Policy (LAW 629-SEM 1).

EQUAL JUSTICE INITIATIVE. **Prison Conditions**. URL: <https://eji.org/issues/prison-conditions/>. Accessed: 1º Apr. 2021.

EWIG V. CALIFORNIA. URL: <https://www.law.cornell.edu/supct/html/01-6978.ZS.html>. Accessed: 1º Apr. 2021.

FARMER V. BRENNAN. URL: <https://supreme.justia.com/cases/federal/us/511/825/>.

FBI - FEDERAL BUREAU OF INFORMATIONS. 2018. Crime in the United States. 2018. URL: <https://ucr.fbi.gov/crime-in-the-u.s/2018/crime-in-the-u.s.-2018/topic-pages/persons-arrested>. Accessed: 7 Apr. 2021.

FISHER, G. **Plea Bargaining's Triumph**: a History of Plea Bargaining in America. California: Stanford University Press, 2004.

FRENZEL, E. D. et al. Understanding Collateral Consequences of Registry Laws: an Examination of the Perceptions of Sex Offender Registrants. **Justice Policy Journal**, n. 11, n. 2 (Fall). URL: <http://www.cjcj.org/uploads/cjcj/documents/frenzel_et_al_collateral_consequences_final_formatted.pdf>. Accessed: 1º Apr. 2021.

GARNER, B. A. **Legal Writing in Plain English**: a Text with Exercises. Second Edition. Chicago: The University of Chicago Press, 2013.

GARNER, B. A. **The Black's Law Dictionary**. ed. 5. Los Angeles: Claitor's Pub Division, 2016.

GOFFMAN, A. **On the run**: Fugitive Life in an American City. Chicago: The University of Chicago Press, 2014.

GROSS, S. Frequency and Predictors of False Conviction: Why We Know So Little, and New Data on Capital Cases. **Journal of Empirical Legal Studies**, n. 927, 2008.

HEALY, J. Wrongfully Convicted Often Find Their Record, Unexpunged, Haunts Them. **New York Times**, May 5, 2013. URL: <https://www.nytimes.com/2013/05/06/us/wrongfully-convicted-find-their-record-haunts-them.html>. Accessed: 1º Apr. 2021.

HANEY, C. **Testimony of Professor Craig Haney Senate Judiciary Subcommittee on the Constitution, Civil Rights, and Human Rights Hearing on Solitary Confinement June 19**, 2012. URL: <https://www.judiciary.senate.gov/imo/media/doc/12-6-19HaneyTestimony.pdf>. Accessed: 1º Apr. 2021.

HEYMANN, P.; PETRI, C. **What's changing in prosecution?: Report of a workshop**. Washington, DC: National Academy Press, 2001.

JACOBS, J. B.; LAURRAUI. E. Are Criminal Convictions a Public Matter? The USA and Spain. **Punishment and Society**, v. 14, ano 1, 2013. URL: <https://journals.sagepub.com/doi/abs/10.1177/1462474511424677>. Accessed: 1º Apr. 2021.

JUSTICE SPEAKER INTERNATIONAL. **Rule Of Law**. URL: <http://www.justicespeakersinternational.com/rule-of-law/#:~:text=The%20laws%20are%20clear%2C%20publicized,is%20accessible%2C%20fair%20and%20efficient>. Accessed: 1º Apr. 2021.

KALACHE, K. V. da R. Plea Bargaining, The Prosecution's Unconstitutional Practices Favoring Efficiency: Negotiating to Broaden Criminal Selectivity. In: SILVA, É. G. da; BRITO, P. de. (Coord.) **Análise Crítica do Direito Público** Íbero-Americano. Porto: Universidade Lusófona do Porto e Instituto Iberoamericano de Estudos Jurídicos, 2020.

KANE, S. **Guide to Law Firm Titles and the Career Ladder**. URL: <https://www.thebalancecareers.com/legal-jobs-part-i-lawyer-careers-2164537>. Accessed: 1º Apr. 2021.

KERR, O. S. How to Read a Judicial Opinion: A Guide for New Law Students. Version 2.0. **George Washington University Law School**, 2005. URL: <http://euro.ecom.cmu.edu/program/law/08-732/Courts/howtoreadv2.pdf>. Accessed: 1º Apr. 2021.

KIRCHMEIER, J. L. Drink, Drugs, and Drowsiness: The Constitutional Right to Effective Assistance of Counsel and the Strickland Prejudice Requirement. **Nebraska Law Review**. v. 75,1996. URL: <https://digitalcommons.unl.edu/nlr/vol75/iss3/3>. Accessed: 1º Apr. 2021.

KROIS-LINDNER, A. TRANSLEGAL. **International Legal English**: A Course for Classroom or Self-Study Use. Cambridge: Cambridge University Press, 2009.

LAW SCHOOL ADMISSION COUNCIL. URL: <https://www.lsac.org/>. Accessed: 1º Apr. 2021.

LIBRARY OF CONGRESS LAW. Fourteenth Amendment and Citinzenship. URL: <https://www.loc.gov/law/help/citizenship/fourteenth_amendment_citizenship.php#:~:text=Citizenship%20is%20defined%20in%20the,the%20State%20wherein%20they%20reside>. Accessed: 1º Apr. 2021.

MAPP V. OHIO. URL: <https://supreme.justia.com/cases/federal/us/367/643/>. Accessed: 7 Apr. 2021.

MIRANDA V. ARIZONA. URL: <https://www.oyez.org/cases/1965/759>. Accessed: 1º Apr. 2021.

MILLER V. ALABAMA. URL: < https://www.law.cornell.edu/supremecourt/text/10-9646>. Accessed: 1º Apr. 2021.NATAPOFF, A. Misdemeanors. **SSRN**, Feb., 2012. URL: <https://ssrn.com/abstract=2010826>. Accessed: 1º Apr. 2021.

NATIONAL CONFERENCE OF STATES LEGISLATURES. URL: <https://www.ncsl.org/research/civil-and-criminal-justice/juvenile-age-of-jurisdictionand-transfer-to-adult-court-laws.aspx>. Accessed: 1º Apr. 2021.

NORTON, J. E. Discovery in the Criminal Process. **The Journal of Criminal Law and Criminology**, v. 61, 1970. URL: <https://scholarlycommons.law.northwestern.edu/jclc/vol61/iss1/2/>. Accessed: 1º Apr. 2021.

PARALEGAL EDU. **Paralegals and Legal Assistants**. URL: <https://www.paralegaledu.org/>. Accessed: 1º Apr. 2021.

PHELPS, M. Mass Probation: Toward a More Robust Theory of State Variation in State Punishment. **Punishment & Society**, May, 2016.

PUBLIC POLICY INSTITUTE OF CALIFORNIA. Alternatives to Incarceration in California, 2015. URL: <https://www.ppic.org/publication/alternatives-to-incarceration-in-california/>. Accessed: 1º Apr. 2021.

RITZ, W. J. Felony Murder, Transferred Intent, And The Palsgraf Doctrine In The Criminal Law. **Washington and Lee University School of Law**, 1959. URL: <https://scholarlycommons.law.wlu.edu/wlulr/vol16/iss2/2>. Accessed: 1º Apr. 2021.

RUIZ V. BROWN. URL: <https://casetext.com/case/ruiz-v-brown-3>. Accessed: 7 Apr. 2021.

SAINATO, M. Why Are So Many People Dying in US Prisons and jails?. **The Guardian**, 2019. URL: <https://www.theguardian.com/us-news/2019/may/26/us-prisons-jails-inmate-deaths>. Accessed: 1º Apr. 2021.

SAWYER, W.; WAGNER, P. Mass Incarceration: The Whole Pie 2020. **Prison Policy Initiative**, 2020. URL: <https://www.prisonpolicy.org/reports/pie2020.html>. Accessed: 1º Apr. 2021.

SEGURA, L. Ohio's Governor Stopped An Execution Over Fears It Would Feel Like Waterboarding. **The Intercept**, 2019. URL: < https://theintercept.com/2019/02/07/death-penalty-lethal-injection-midazolam-ohio/>. Accessed: 1º Apr. 2021.

STRICKLAND V. WASHINGTON. URL: <https://supreme.justia.com/cases/federal/us/466/668/>. Accessed: 7 Apr. 2021.

TAIBBI; M. **The Divide**: American Injustice in the Age of the Wealth Gap. 1. ed. New York: Spiegel & Grau: 2014.

TATE V. SHORT. URL: <https://supreme.justia.com/cases/federal/us/401/395/>. Accessed: 7 Apr. 2021.

TAXMAN, F., S. Probation, Intermediate Sanctions, and Community-Based Correction. In: PETERSILIA, J.; REITZ, K. R. **The Oxford Handbook of Sentencing and Corrections**. New York: Oxford University Press, 2012.

THE CONSTITUTION OF THE UNITED STATES OF AMERICA. URL: <https://www.senate.gov/civics/resources/pdf/US_Constitution-Senate_Publication_103-21.pdf>. Accessed: 1º Apr. 2021.

THE CONSEQUENCES OF CRIMINAL PROCEEDINGS IN NY STATE. A Guide for Criminal Defense Attorneys and Other Advocates for Persons with Criminal Records, 2015. URL: <https://www.reentry.net/ny/search/attachment.265297+&cd=1&hl=pt-BR&ct=clnk&gl=br>. Accessed: 1º Apr. 2021.

UNIVERSITY OF CHICAGO. **The Socratic Method**. URL: <https://www.law.uchicago.edu/socratic-method>. Accessed: 1º Apr. 2021.

UNITED STATES DEPARTMENT OF JUSTICE. Steps in the Federal Criminal Process. URL: <https://www.justice.gov/usao/justice-101/steps-federal-criminal-process>. Accessed: 1º Apr. 2021.

WACQUANT, L. **As prisões da miséria**. Tradução de André Telles. 2. ed. Rio de Janeiro: Zahar, 2011.

WILSON V. SEITER. URL: <https://supreme.justia.com/cases/federal/us/501/294/>. Accessed: 7 Apr. 2021.WONSOVICZ, P. **Evidence**: a Context and Practice Casebook. 2. ed. Durham: Carolina Academic Press, 2017.

About the author

Kauana Vieira da Rosa Kalache holds a bachelor's degree in Law from the Pontifícia Universidade Católica do Paraná (Brazil, 2011), a specialization degree in Criminal Law and Criminology from the Instituto de Criminologia e Políticas Criminais (Brazil, 2014) and a Master of Law (Legum Magister – LL.M) in Criminal Law from the University of California – Ucla (United States, 2015). She is currently enrolled at the full scholarship master's program from the Centro Universitário Internacional – Uninter (Brazil, 2019-2020).

She is a law professor and practices law as a criminal defender.

Os papéis utilizados neste livro, certificados por instituições ambientais competentes, são recicláveis, provenientes de fontes renováveis e, portanto, um meio **respons**ável e natural de informação e conhecimento.

MISTO
Papel produzido a partir de fontes responsáveis
FSC® C103535

Impressão: Reproset
Fevereiro/2023